Heroes of God

DAN AND KATIE MONTGOMERY

ILLUSTRATED BY
LYDIA HALVERSON

Augsburg
MINNEAPOLIS

Family Read-Aloud Collection
Foreword by Walter Wangerin, Jr.

VOL. IV

Cover design by Craig P. Claeys
Text design by Lois Stanfield, LightSource Images

Library of Congress Cataloging-in-Publication Data

Montgomery, Dan, 1946-
      Heroes of God / Dan and Katie Montgomery : illustrated by Lydia Halverson.
          p.   cm. — (Family read-aloud collection ; vol. 4)
      Summary: Fifteen stories of men and women of long ago whose lives and deeds
reflected the Christian virtues of faith, love, and honor. Includes Hildegard of
Bingen, Leonardo da Vinci, and Louis Braille.
      ISBN 0-8066-3607-6 (alk. paper)
      1. Christian biography—Juvenile literature.   [1. Christian biography.]
I. Montgomery, Katie, 1941- . II. Halverson, Lydia, ill. III. Title.
IV. Series.
BR1704.M66 1998
270'.092'2—dc21
[B]   98-21256
                                                                                    CIP
                                                                                    AC

The paper used in this publication meets the minimum requirements of American
National Standard for Information Sciences—Permanence of Paper for Printed
Library Materials, ANSI Z329.48-1984.

Manufactured in Hong Kong   AF 9-3607

02   01   00   99   98   1   2   3   4   5   6   7   8   9   10

Contents

FOREWORD

Worlds to Share

WALTER WANGERIN, JR.

ow often I wished I could companion my children through their most difficult experiences—or through their every joy. Too often I learned of the twists of their personal journeys after the fact. I hadn't been there. Moreover, if I had been, I may have been denied full access to—a full understanding of—their hearts and minds in the event.

But there is a way, a blessed way, into the hearts and minds of our children as they journey through life. When the parent reads out loud to the child, the older one becomes the younger one's most intimate companion. They travel together through dangers and delights, through adventures and mysteries, through stories, through genuine experiences—through life itself.

The power of a story well told is to create whole experiences for the child, but controlled experiences with beginnings and middles, and with good endings.

The reward for parents who read such stories to their children is an intimacy that is emotional, spiritual, and real. The walls come down; nothing is hidden between them.

And the benefits to children are legion:

- They are assured that, whatever the experience, they are not alone.

- They are fearless before the circumstances of the story, however frightening or thrilling. And, in consequence, they are prepared to meet similar circumstances in their real life with the boldness and trust that come of experience.

- They, when they laugh heartily, are empowered! For the laughter of children in the face of giants or troubles or evils is their sense of superiority. Their ability to see silliness in danger is their freedom to take spiritual steps above the danger.

- And they are granted a genuine independence, a freedom of choice. For children can choose to hear a fantasy tale as fantasy only, something fun and funny, but not anything you would meet in the real world. And they can listen to stories of distant heroes and heroic deeds as ancient history and nothing to do with their life. Or else they can choose to identify completely with the main character—in which case this fantasy or this ancient story stands for things absolutely real in their own world. Children don't make such choices consciously; they make them in the deep parts of their souls, when they are ready to take the real ride of the story. And the fact that they can and do choose grants them true personhood.

And you, their parent, are there, companioning your child through wonders and terrors, through friendships and wisdom, through experience into experience.

When my father bought a thick book containing all the tales of Hans Christian Andersen and read them to us, he did me a kindness more profound than mere entertainment. He began to weave a world that genuinely acknowledged all the monsters in mine, as well as all the ridiculous situations and silly asides that I as a child found significant. Dad/Andersen was my whispering, laughing, wise companion when I most needed companionship.

Night after night my dad would read a story in his articulate, baritone voice. Gently the voice invited me. Slowly I accepted the invitation and delivered myself to a wonderful world. And as I looked around, I discovered that this world was confident with solutions, and I was a citizen of some authority and reputation. I was no longer alone, no longer helpless.

Dad would sit in a chair beside my bed, one lamp low at his shoulder, his pipe clamped between his teeth and sending the smell of his presence and his affections to me where I lay. Mostly the room, an attic with slanted ceilings, was in darkness. The wind whistled in the eaves.

"Ready?" Dad would say.

We would nod. We would curl tight beneath the covers.

"Once upon a time," Dad would read, sending me straight through the attic walls into the night, onto the wind, for gorgeous, breathtaking flights.

What part of my being could not find affirmation in such an event? My body was present, delighting in its vicarious adventures. All my senses were alert and active, sight and sound and smell and touch. My emotions were given every opportunity—highs so tremendously high, and lows acceptable because Dad was the leader. My mind, my intellect, labored at solutions before the story itself declared them.

And all my affections were granted lovely objects. I could love in that event when my father read to us: I could love characters in the tale; I could love their qualities, their deeds, their struggles; I could love the tale itself—but mostly, I could love my father, whose very voice was his offering of love to me. We were one in this event, one in the reading and in the listening and in the experiencing.

Night after night my father read to us from that thick book. Night after night I lived the adventures that gave order to my turbulent child's experience. The tales gave shape to my waking self, to my instincts, to my faith in God, and to my adulthood yet to come. For I am what I am now, in part, because once I experienced important events within the protected sphere of my father's dear influence.

These events were deep and primal.

But on the page they were merely stories—until my father opened his mouth and read them to me.

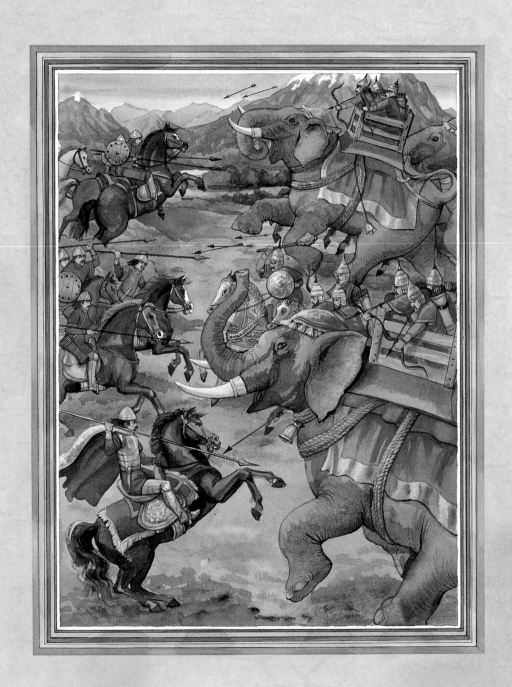

The Prince and the Persians

VARDAN MAMIKONIAN
A.D. 451

I n 451, Christianity was still new to the world. Armenia, a small Middle Eastern country south of Persia, had recently become Christian. To celebrate their new faith, Armenian Christians built beautiful churches.

But the powerful country of Persia (called Iran today) ruled Armenia, as well as many of its other small neighbors. The Persian religion, Zoroastrianism (zohr-oh-WASS-tree-un-izm) was very different from Christianity.

The king of Persia ordered the Armenians to give up Christianity for the Persian religion. He sent his priests to Armenia to enforce his command. But the Armenians would not give up their faith. Finally, the king sent a huge army to Armenia. All Christian churches were to be destroyed. Any men who refused to give up Christianity would be put to death, and their wives and children would be cast out of the kingdom.

The Armenians decided to defy the Persian king. The leader of the small band of men who faced Persia's great army was Prince Vardan (VAHR-dun) Mamikonian (Mam-ih-KOHN-yun).

PRINCE VARDAN HUNCHED OVER in concentration, studying the words of the Bible on his table. Light and shadows from his campfire flickered across the paper.

"Almighty God," he prayed, "guide me to inspire the troops in battle tomorrow. The Persians outnumber us four to one. They will slaughter us without your help. Save us so that we can keep worshiping your Son, and so that our children can have the same freedom!"

Vardan heard a movement behind him and glanced around. An officer snapped to attention. He held something under his left arm.

"Your cloak, my Prince," said the major, holding out Vardan's gold-trimmed cloak—the cloak that marked him as a general. "The men are assembling to hear you speak, sir."

"Well done, Major," Vardan replied. He put the Bible away, stood up, and clasped the wool cloak around his shoulders. Prince Vardan towered over the major as well as over most other soldiers in his army.

Vardan watched the troops gather around a huge campfire on the plain. The cool evening breeze swirled the folds of his cloak and sent a chill down his spine. *Will tomorrow bring victory or death to all these men? he wondered.*

Vardan knew his troops were well-trained, yet how could 66,000 men face a Persian army of 220,000? It would be like David facing Goliath.

A young captain ran up to Vardan's tent and saluted crisply. "They're ready for you, General." The prince whispered a final prayer and strode purposefully down the hill to the main campfire. A sea of soldiers parted as he made his way to a platform in the middle of camp.

Vardan climbed the platform, took a deep breath, and gazed out at the waiting faces.

"You men know why we are here," Vardan's deep voice rang out. A chorus of agreement rippled through the army. The prince felt another chill, this time of inspiration. "The Persians forbid us to worship Jesus Christ," he bellowed. "What do you say to this?"

"No! We will never give in!" Angry shouts of protest erupted from the crowd.

"At other times men have fought for the right to worship the one true God," Vardan continued. "The Jewish Maccabees (MACK-uh-beez) fought against the tyrant Antiochus (an-TIE-uh-kus). They wanted freedom to worship the God of Abraham, Isaac, and Jacob. Many gave their lives for that freedom."

The troops listened in rapt silence as Vardan told them how the Maccabees led a victorious revolt against the tyrant king.

"And now," shouted Vardan, "for the first time in history, we Christians are fighting a battle to keep our religion and pass it to our children!"

Men raised their fists and thundered their approval.

Vardan waited until they grew quiet. "Tomorrow we face a force many times our size. We know that they are heavily armed, and we know of their trained war elephants. But we know even more that God is with us. Those of us who die will be greeted in heaven by the Lord Jesus himself. The Lord will champion our cause. We proclaim that Christ is Lord and Savior!"

The men pounded spears on the ground and crashed swords against shields like cymbals. "Christ is Lord!" they shouted.

Vardan looked out at the faithful men, knowing he would see many of them next in heaven. Then he raised his fist to the sky and cried out, "The battle is the Lord's!"

The next morning as an early mist was lifting, Prince Vardan eyed the great plain of Avaryar (AV-ur-yahr) stretching out before him. Far off to his left, the Tigris River flowed through deep gorges and steep canyons. On his right loomed mighty Mount Ararat (AIR-uh-rat), its snow-covered peak the supposed resting place of Noah's ark. "Lord," prayed Vardan, "give me the courage of Noah."

Across the plain stood his soldiers holding the gold and wine-colored flags of the Armenian army. Behind him he could hear the cavalry horses snort and paw the ground, sensing the battle to come.

As Vardan rode back and forth inspecting the troops, his armor and helmet glistened in the sun. Line upon line of foot-soldiers hefted heavy spears as the men formed up behind the cavalry. The archers fell into ranks in the rear.

Vardan spurred his tall black horse to the head of the troops. While other military leaders preferred to observe the fighting from the safety of nearby hills, Vardan personally led his men into battle.

A mile away loomed the massive Persian army. Hundreds of thousands of enemy soldiers flooded the distant plain, their green and red flags fluttering in the breeze. Heat waves rising from the earth made the Persians look like shimmering ghosts.

Prince Vardan wheeled his horse around to face his troops, who were silently staring out across the plain. He struggled for words to speak, words that could stir the men's spirits for battle against such a force. "Lord, give us courage!" he whispered.

A surge of faith welled up inside him, and Vardan thrust his gleaming sword into the air, shouting, "Victory! Victory for God and for Armenia!"

A deafening roar erupted as his troops echoed the battle cry. Vardan turned to face the enemy and spurred his horse to a full gallop. The cavalry charged on his heels, raising their swords with fierce shouts. Foot soldiers and archers followed the charge.

Moments later the battle of Avaryar was raging. Sword clanged against sword and spears hissed through the air. Arrows rained from the skies. Cries of triumph, agony, and death resounded across the plain.

As the day wore on, Persian and Armenian losses mounted. Vardan rode in the thick of the fighting, wielding his sword and urging his men on. A Persian officer stabbed the prince's leg but was killed an instant later by one of Vardan's foot soldiers.

Suddenly a series of trumpet calls blasted from the Persian ranks. Prince Vardan looked up to see dozens of war elephants lumbering onto the battlefield. Persian bowmen stood in iron towers strapped to the top of the beasts. From this great height, the archers fired deadly arrows down at Vardan's fighters. Persian soldiers surrounded the elephants, defending them from attack.

The Armenian troops hurled spears at these new attackers, but few reached their target from such a distance. Scores of Vardan's soldiers fell as the Persian archers continued their onslaught.

His dark eyes flashing fury, Vardan assembled ten of his remaining officers. "Pull your cavalry back and attack from the rear," he shouted. "I will charge from the front with the remaining foot soldiers. Onward! May God be with you!"

While the officers regrouped their men and galloped around to the rear of the Persians, Prince Vardan led an infantry charge straight into the center of the enemy. The fighting was fierce and bloody. Vardan could see his troops gaining ground as thousands of Persians perished. But the cost was great: Many of Vardan's infantry and cavalry had fallen as well.

Then, at the height of the battle, Vardan turned to fend off a sword, and a Persian arrow pierced his neck. As his vision began to blur, he gasped, "Jesus, receive my spirit. And give victory to my people!"

Prince Vardan fell from his black horse into the arms of heaven.

*T*he battle of Avaryar was fought on June 2, 451. Although Prince Vardan was killed and the Persians won the battle, so many Persian soldiers were slain that their king gave up his goal of making Armenians change their religion. It was Vardan's leadership and courage that eventually led to freedom for Armenia.

Prince Vardan Mamikonian, "the Brave," is numbered among the saints of the Armenian church. The anniversary of the Battle of Avaryar is one of its main festivals.

Talk about It

- Vardan and his soldiers fought to the death for freedom to worship as they pleased. What kind of threats or dangers to our faith do we face today? Would our religion mean more to us if we had to fight for it, like the ancient Armenians?

- Is it important to allow other people freedom to believe and worship as they please—even when their religion is different from ours? Or should we try to pressure them to believe as we do? How can we respect religious views that are different from ours while standing up for our own?

Prayer

Dear Lord, we pray for your guidance and protection against those who might turn us away from you by things they say or do. Give us wisdom and courage to stand firm in our faith, give us kindness and understanding toward those who do not believe as we do. We know you are our ready help in time of trouble. Thank you. Amen.

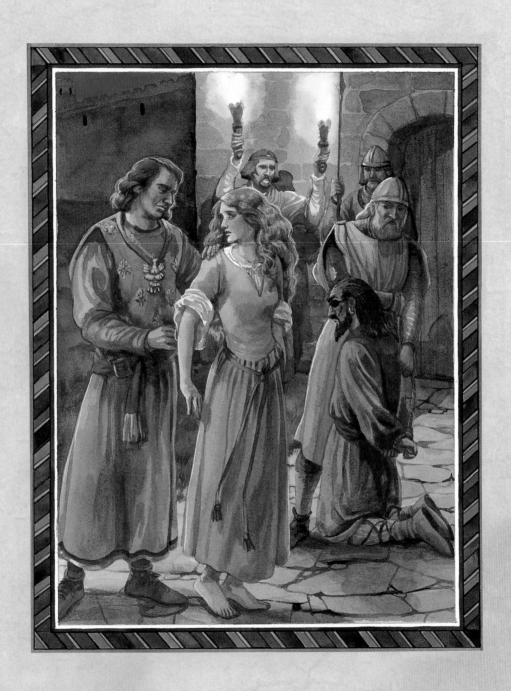

The Slave Girl and the Pirates

BATHILDIS
A.D. 680

athildis (bah-TIL-dis) was a Christian girl who lived near-ly two thousand years ago on the southern coast of England. Her family tended a tiny farm near the channel of water sep-arating England from France.

One morning Bathildis was kidnapped from her home. A band of pirates stole in from the coast and seized the girl, taking her across the sea to a part of France ruled by King Clovis II.

In those days, many poor young people were kidnapped from England and sold into slavery—some as far away as Rome. Back then, France was not united. Kings and nobles fought to control different regions. Clovis ruled an area that included what is now the city of Paris.

The king lived in luxury. He and his nobles hunted—both for food and for sport. They ate well and wore fine clothing. They also provided money to Christian priests for building churches and monasteries. In contrast, peasant farmers lived in poverty. They built crude huts and spent their lives clearing enough land to grow crops for food.

It was to King Clovis's castle that Bathildis was brought as a slave.

EIGHTEEN-YEAR-OLD BATHILDIS stood in the linen room at the end of a hallway, carefully folding sheets for the royal bedchambers.

Suddenly she heard a commotion in the courtyard one floor below. She stepped into the hallway and looked out the small window. Some rough-looking men had arrived on horseback. She gasped as she recognized the leader, who wore a black patch over one eye. Even from this distance, she could make out a long scar on his cheek.

He's one of the pirates who brought me here two years ago, she said to herself. What are they doing here now?

Bathildis hurried back into the linen room and shut the door. "Dear God," she prayed, "please save me from harm!"

In the dark room, she trembled with fear as she recalled her kidnapping. She had just come home from Sunday mass and was preparing to milk the cow. Out of nowhere, a pair of rough hands grabbed her from behind and slipped a blindfold over her eyes. A hand closed over her mouth, muffling her screams. Within moments she was heaved onto a horse and held tightly as the pirates galloped away.

The next afternoon the blindfold was taken off. Bright sun stung her eyes as she looked around. About fifty of her country-men, including several youths her age, were being led up a gang-plank to a ship. The kidnappers were frightening men with scrag-gly beards, tattered clothing, and knives in their belts.

The leader had a black patch over one eye and a long scar on his cheek. "Heave ho, laddies!" he yelled. "Let's be out of here before the English send a rescue party. Don't want to lose our special cargo!"

They sailed all night as high waves rocked the ship. Many peo-ple got seasick. Bathildis held a younger girl in her arms who sobbed throughout the night.

"Jesus," Bathildis had prayed, "please protect all of these poor people. When I grow up, help me to free people like us who have been kidnapped and taken from their families."

At sunrise the next morning, the ship arrived in port. Bathildis heard someone whisper that they were in France. The people were herded off the ship and sold as slaves.

"I'll take the brown-haired girl with the green eyes," called an old man wearing a red cloak. He was pointing at Bathildis. "She's a beauty—fit for the castle of King Clovis."

Bathildis learned that this man was in charge of the castle servants. As the two of them made the long journey to King Clovis's castle, the castle manager told her, not unkindly: "Do what you're told and you won't be mistreated." Bathildis felt numb. Her heart ached for her family and homeland.

Bathildis shook her head to erase the unhappy memory. She crept from the linen room and peeked out the window again. No sign of the pirates. *Did they bring new slaves with them?* she wondered. *Oh, dear, I hope they won't be eating in the great hall tonight.*

At King Clovis's request, the castle manager had selected Bathildis to serve at a royal banquet that night. The king had noticed this beautiful young girl who served him with such skill and pride.

She had been looking forward to the banquet until the pirates arrived. Now she felt afraid.

Suddenly a trumpet blared. She looked down from the window to see the king and his nobles arrive from their afternoon hunt. Bathildis watched King Clovis. He seems so gentle, she thought. Not like his nobles who are often cruel. The king always had a kind word for those who showed loyalty to him—even servants.

Bathildis heard footsteps coming down the corridor. "The pirates!" she whispered, huddling against the wall. Then there was a familiar, low whistle.

"Marta!" she exclaimed as the castle seamstress rounded the corner. Marta took care of all the sewing in the castle. She was plump and cheerful and was Bathildis's best friend.

"Whatever is the matter, Bathildis?" asked Marta. "You look as white as the sheet in your hands."

"It's the pirates," whispered Bathildis. "I saw them ride up a while ago. It was one of them who kidnapped me!"

"Oh, you poor thing," consoled Marta, taking Bathildis into her arms. "Those rascals are down in the kitchen eating everything in sight and getting drunk on ale and wine."

"Did they bring slaves from England?" asked Bathildis.

"Yes," Marta replied quietly. "Three young men your age. The castle manager sent them to work in the stables."

"Oh," cried Bathildis, forgetting her fear. "God help me, if I can ever set slaves free, I will!"

Marta nodded sympathetically then smiled. She pulled out a green wool dress that was tucked under her arm.

"Here is the dress I promised to make for you. You can wear it tonight. But you must hurry. The castle manager told me he wants you down early in the great hall. You'll be serving at the king's own table!"

The two women stepped into the linen room where Bathildis slipped into the dress.

"Now hurry," said Marta. "You mustn't be late."

Just in time, Bathildis joined the other servants who were bowing as the king and his guests strode into the great hall.

The hall was enormous, with long wooden tables forming a square in the middle. Two huge fireplaces warmed the room and cast flickering light and shadows across the tables.

The pirates were nowhere to be seen. Bathildis breathed a sigh of relief. She carefully poured wine into the king's jeweled goblet, making sure to spill none on his fine blue robe. A heavy ruby necklace glittered on the king's chest as he leaned back. At that moment, his eyes met Bathildis's, and she immediately looked down.

"Bathildis, I am well pleased with the service you give your king," he said.

He knows my name, she thought, blushing. "Th–thank you, Your Majesty," she stammered.

"My castle manager tells me you have done much to improve the running of my household," he continued.

"I try to do my best, my lord," Bathildis replied. She curtsied and moved away.

After the banquet was over, Bathildis helped clean the great hall. It was late when she made her way to her room, carrying a candle to light her way through the dark hallways. She felt tired, but the king's words echoed in her ears and thrilled her.

Suddenly she heard a movement—a footstep—somewhere behind her. She looked back, holding out the candle.

"Who's there?" asked Bathildis. "Marta, is that you?"

There was silence. Then a dark shadow moved toward her. Too late Bathildis jumped back in fear. A powerful hand seized her arm.

"Not so fast, pretty girl," growled a familiar voice. His sour breath reeked of wine.

Bathildis pushed her candle into his face and felt his grip loosen as he howled in pain. She bolted down the hall and ran into the courtyard screaming for help.

Within moments guards surrounded her. She pointed to the hallway. "In there!" she yelled. "A man attacked me!"

Two guards disappeared into the castle and returned shortly with the scar-faced pirate who was struggling and cursing.

"Is this the man?" a guard asked.

"Yes. That's him," said Bathildis firmly.

A deep voice spoke from behind them: "Take him away. Jail him!" King Clovis strode up to the group.

He placed a gentle hand on Bathildis's shoulder. "You will never see that man again," he said quietly. "Did he harm you?"

"No, my lord," she said. "I am learning how to protect myself."

"You have a brave heart, Bathildis," said the king warmly. "And you will have a good future, so help me God."

At mass the next morning, Bathildis gave thanks to God for her rescue. After breakfast, the king sent a servant to bring her to his throne room.

As Bathildis bowed, the king took her hand and gently led her to a window seat looking out over the courtyard. "Please sit here beside me," he said. "I've been aware of you for some time now, Bathildis. You have a ready smile for everyone, and you are trustworthy in all your responsibilities."

"Thank you, Your Majesty." Bathildis blushed with pleasure.

"Beyond that, you are a lovely young woman, Bathildis, and possess all the qualities I would like in a wife." The king took both her hands in his. "Will you be my queen?"

Bathildis felt a surge of joy. She looked into the king's eyes and declared, "Yes, my lord. I will be honored to marry you."

The day before their wedding, the king gave Bathildis a silver and sapphire necklace and a gold and ruby necklace. "These are yours, my Bathildis, to do with as you please," he told her.

The marriage was celebrated quietly in the castle chapel. Nobles and servants looked on as a priest blessed the couple. Clovis placed a gold ring on her finger and pronounced Bathildis his queen.

Several weeks later Queen Bathildis was riding with her husband in the royal forest. "Do you remember what you said about the jewels you gave me?" she asked.

"Of course," he said. "They are yours to do with as you please."

"I would like to use them to buy freedom for the English people who were kidnapped by pirates and made slaves. And whatever money may be left over will be used to pay their passage home."

Clovis smiled and leaned from his saddle to take her hand. "My kind-hearted queen!" he said. "Your requests are granted."

Bathildis bowed her head as she remembered her prayer to God from the pirates' ship long years ago. God answered my prayer, she thought. He set me free and gave me power to free others.

King Clovis and Queen Bathildis had three sons. Clovis died when the oldest son was only five years old. Bathildis ruled the kingdom until her son was old enough to take the throne. She was kind to poor people and helped free many who had been slaves. She built hospitals, a seminary for priests, and a convent. Before she died, Bathildis entered a convent and took orders from the mother superior. Even though she was a queen, she never forsook her gentle Christian ways.

Talk about It

- Even though people are Christians, bad things can happen to them. What, then, is the good of faith in God—especially in times of trouble or danger?

Prayer

Dear Jesus, please bring your power and wisdom to our family when bad things happen to any of us. Give us wisdom and faith to believe that you are with us in those times. And help us use our talents wisely—no matter where we are—and let you take care of the results.

The Dancing Nuns

HILDEGARD OF BINGEN
1098–1179

Hildegard was the tenth child of a noble Christian family in Germany. Raised on a large estate in rolling green farmland, Hildegard spent her early years surrounded by the beauty of nature.

As was common for noble families, two of Hildegard's brothers became priests, and one sister became a nun. But little Hildegard seemed to have an even deeper closeness to God. At the age of three, she reported her first of many visions from God. She would be sitting quietly or be about to go to sleep when beautiful sights would appear in her mind's eye. When she continued having these visions, her family sent her with an aunt to live in a convent. Hildegard grew in her love for God and, when she was older, became a nun.

A strong-willed woman, Hildegard had unusual power for a woman of her time. Her spiritual visions were treated with respect by the clergy and pope. She was eventually chosen to be abbess, or leader, of the convent she founded.

HILDEGARD LAY MOTIONLESS ON THE BED of her room in the convent, waiting until the wave of pain passed from her body. Thankful to feel it leave, she opened her eyes but saw only darkness. *I can't see,* she thought as blackness swirled around her. She closed her eyes tightly, and her lips moved in prayer: "Dear God, help me!"

Gradually her anxiety eased. A peace swept through her that she felt as strongly as she had felt the pain. At the age of twenty-five, she again sensed the friendly Presence that had accompanied the visions of her childhood. Her eyes still closed, she saw a shimmering white light with images forming inside it.

In this vision, a group of young women were standing on green grass within a radiant light. Near them was a garden of red and blue flowers. Hildegard could smell the sweet-scented blossoms. The young maidens wore long white gowns fastened with belts of gold and pearls. On their heads rested golden crowns with sparkling diamonds and red rubies. Their gowns were embroidered with lilies and roses.

The young women sang joyfully to melodies they plucked on golden harps. Although she couldn't understand their words, Hildegard somehow knew they were singing about their love for Jesus, the Lamb of God. At times the women seemed to hover in the air, their silver slippers dancing on wheels of gold.

When their song ended, Hildegard's vision grew dim then disappeared. She lay still, drinking in the vision's afterglow and puzzling about its meaning.

Hesitantly, Hildegard opened her eyes and saw rays of sunlight streaming through a solitary window. The tiny room contained a bed, stool, and wooden chest. The nun glanced at a picture of Jesus that hung over the wooden chest. The Lord seemed to be smiling at her with a question in his eyes.

Although everyone in the convent knew about Hildegard's visions, she had not yet shared this particular one. Not even with her best friend, Richardis (ri-KAR-dis). *Why am I afraid to ask God what this vision means?* she asked herself. *And why does it keep appearing to me?*

Hildegard got out of bed and slipped on the long black robe and veil she kept folded in the chest. *I've got to get on with my chores,* she thought. Walking down the corridor toward the dining hall, she ran into another black-robed young woman.

"Hildegard," her friend called out, "you are up and well again. Praise be to God! I was just coming to check on you."

Hildegard smiled. "Thank you, Richardis. I felt faint for a while and couldn't see. But now I'm okay. After morning prayer and breakfast, I intend to weed the vegetable garden."

Later that morning, Hildegard pinched out weeds from a row of freshly sprouting herbs. More than almost anything, she loved tending the vegetables and herbs in the convent's garden. She sniffed the aroma of rich loamy soil, then suddenly she felt sick to her stomach. Holding a hand over her mouth, she hurried toward the convent kitchen. Bertha, one of the cooks, ran to her.

"Here, Sister," Bertha said, guiding Hildegard to a chair. "You're up and about too early, I'd say. Likely you're weakened from the visions the good Lord sends you. Let's walk back to your room, and I'll send Sister Richardis to tend to you."

Back in the coolness of her room, Hildegard lay on her bed while Richardis dabbed a damp cloth over her forehead. The wetness felt soothing. After a few minutes, Richardis sat back on the stool and looked thoughtfully at Hildegard.

"Now, suppose you tell me what is going on with you, Sister Hildegard," Richardis said.

Hildegard kept silent, and Richardis continued. "Over the past weeks, you've kept to yourself more than usual. Maybe your illness is telling you that you need to talk to someone."

A few moments later, Hildegard pulled the cloth from her brow and gazed at Richardis. "You're right," she sighed. "I've been avoiding you." She sat up and looked at the painting of Jesus on the wall. "And I've been avoiding the Lord, too."

Richardis leaned forward.

"You see," said Hildegard softly, "I've had a strange vision. Three times God has brought it to me. It is so vivid. So moving. Yet I'm afraid to ask God what it means."

Hildegard paused then blurted out, "I haven't told anyone about it because I'm afraid God is asking me to do something that is too difficult."

"Why don't you ask the Lord what the vision means right now?" encouraged Richardis. "I'll stay with you until he answers."

Hildegard nodded her head, breathed deeply, and closed her eyes. "Dear Father, please tell me the meaning of the vision with the singing maidens. I am ready now to hear your answer."

Richardis, too, prayed with hands folded and head bowed. A peaceful silence filled the room while the two friends waited.

Finally, Hildegard opened her eyes and looked at Richardis. "I am to tell you and the other sisters that we must create a new place to live." With excitement and awe in her voice, Hildegard continued, "And God has chosen me to be the leader of this convent. All who join us are to seek a closer walk with God by growing closer to God's world."

Richardis lifted her eyebrows, trying to take in this new idea. "How are we supposed to do that?" she asked.

Hildegard beamed, for suddenly she knew the answer in her heart. "We are to use more of our senses—touch, sight, smell, taste, and hearing—to know Jesus." She spoke eagerly. "We are to develop music and song, painting, writing, and the reading and study of Scripture. We will find that these creative things bring us closer to the Lord, who is Creator of all!" She looked down at her black robe. "And we are to exchange these dull black robes for white ones. The Lord wants us clothed in robes that are bright and joyous. We are brides of the Lamb of God. Now I understand that the maidens in my vision are dancing nuns!"

Richardis, caught up in Hildegard's enthusiasm, cried out, "Oh, yes! We can celebrate our love for Jesus through the senses he gave us." Then she grew quiet and gently touched Hildegard's arm. "This will bring big changes to the sisters here. And the Lord has put you in charge!"

Courage welling up within her, Hildegard said, "Yes, but with a friend like you by my side and the Holy Spirit guiding, how can I fail?" She sprang out of bed and hugged Richardis. "Let's share the vision with Mother Superior first and see if she will permit me to tell the other sisters tonight."

The two nuns hurried out of the bedroom and down the hallway to the mother superior. In their hearts, they were already singing as joyfully as the maidens in Hildegard's shimmering vision.

Several years later, Hildegard and the nuns who had joined her new community were flourishing in a convent near Rupertsburg, Germany.

One sunny morning after chapel and breakfast, Hildegard walked out to tend the herbs sheltered in a corner of the convent garden. She eyed with approval the purple lavender edging the herbs and then snipped several sprigs of bright yellow marigolds. From these the nuns would make healing ointments for skin wounds. She collected a few other herbs for the healing of other illnesses.

That evening the sisters gathered on a grassy hill. The fragrance of lilies and roses filled the air. Birds in nearby trees chirped their evening songs. The setting sun cast a pink glow across a band of clouds.

It was Hildegard's turn to offer a meditation from the Bible. She had set to music a text from the book of Revelation. She hummed the tune until the sisters joined in, accompanied by several nuns who strummed harps. Hildegard sang the verses, with everyone singing along on the chorus: "Blessed are those who are invited to the marriage supper of the Lamb!"

The nuns swayed back and forth worshiping the Lord for the next hour. Long white robes swirled and feet tapped out rhythms, dancing like wheels of light over the green grass.

Hildegard smiled from ear to ear, while her inner eye fixed on the approving face of Jesus.

Hildegard is known not only for her visions from God, but also for her knowledge of herbal medicine, her music compositions, and her dramas. She wrote books on theology, poetry, music, and several dealing with her spiritual visions.

Traveling around the countryside, Hildegard preached in many cathedrals about the love of God. She warned clergy to give up their interest in property and wealth, and replace it with purity of heart by following Jesus. Hildegard challenged both church and state about the belief that society should be run and ruled solely by men.

Today, the study of her inspired visions and music is enjoying a popular rebirth in the marketplace throughout the world.

Talk about It

- Why is it important to use all of our senses in worshiping God? Become aware of the setting that surrounds your family now. Feel the texture of things around you. Close your eyes and listen to the sounds you hear. How might these sights, sounds, and textures bring you closer to God?

- Share any vision or dream you have had that you think could be God-given.

Prayer

Jesus, help us use all our senses and the beauty of nature to know and love you better and to appreciate the world you have given us.

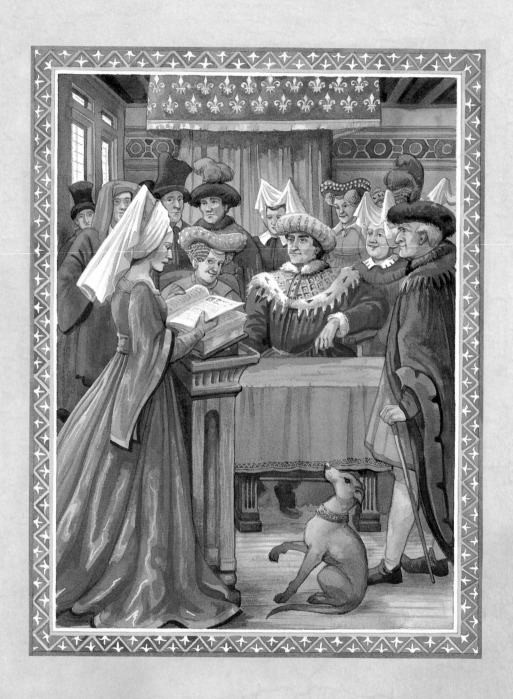

The City of Ladies

CHRISTINE DE PISAN
1365–1430

C hristine de Pisan (pee-ZAHN) lived in Paris over six hundred years ago. Paris society was controlled by the king and the church. Women were seen as physically and emotionally unsuitable to hold positions of power.

As a child, Christine was fortunate to have had a father who encouraged her interest in learning. Christine had a happy marriage, but her husband died, stranding her at the age of twenty-five with three children to support. Responding to the need for income and her interest in expressing ideas, she became the first professional female writer in France.

Christine's main interest was writing about women's rights. She believed that a correct understanding of Christianity would overcome negative attitudes toward women. After all, she wrote, Adam was just as guilty as Eve in bringing sin into the world. And it was women who remained faithful to Jesus during his trial and death. Contrary to many churchmen's views, she asserted, many women were intelligent as well as gentle and loving. With these ideas in mind, she wrote a book about a city whose only inhabitants were ladies.

WEARING A RED SILK DRESS and a pointed white headdress, Christine swept into an elegant Paris living room, her latest book tucked under her arm. The city's wealthy nobles had gathered to hear her read from her book *The City of Ladies*.

Counts and countesses came dressed in high fashion. Dukes and duchesses arrived in carriages. Knowing the power of these people, Christine feared that if they didn't like her story, they could destroy her writing career.

Christine sat down in a silk-covered chair and prayed, "Dear God, let my words serve you tonight." Then she carefully opened the manuscript. Christine had spent long hours learning the art of beautiful handwriting. Each page was filled with gracefully drawn letters and illustrations for her story.

The hum of conversation among the lords and ladies died down as she stood.

"My lords and ladies," Christine said as she curtsied, "I thank you for your presence this evening. I humbly present to you a story from my book *The City of Ladies*."

Here is the story Christine read to the French nobility:

Once upon a time, there was a city built especially for ladies. This city was surrounded with walls of white marble. Three queens lived in a castle with graceful crystal towers. The city's church was filled for every service, and those who spoke were ladies. The ladies lived in comfortable homes constructed for warmth in the winter and coolness in the summer. Trees lined the streets, and scented flowers blossomed in grassy parks.

One day, a young lady named Marguerite asked for permission to visit the three queens. She needed their advice.

Her request was approved, and the following morning Marguerite walked through the gates into the City of Ladies. She was greeted by a lady-in-waiting who led Marguerite to the door of the crystal castle and then to the throne room of the queens.

Three queens wearing crowns of gold sat on emerald thrones. A red carpet covered the marble floor in front of them. Red satin chairs faced the thrones. One of the queens gestured for Marguerite to sit down.

"Please ask us your questions, Marguerite," one of them said.

"Why are there three queens?" Marguerite asked.

"Because each of us represents a quality needed for a good life," said one. "I am Queen Reason." She stood and held up a mirror in her right hand, its frame glistening with silver. "I always carry this mirror so people can see their real selves when they look into it. If they stray from being true to themselves, the mirror shows them right behavior."

The second Queen stood up. She held a ruler carved of black ebony and edged with ivory. "I am Queen Honesty," she said. "I hold a ruler that measures right and wrong."

The third queen arose. She held a balancing scale made from mother-of-pearl. "I am Queen Justice," she announced. "I am fair-minded and give out rewards or punishments depending on what people deserve." She sat down again and smiled at Marguerite. "Now what has brought you here, my dear?"

"A rich nobleman named Pierre has asked my father's permission to marry me," said Marguerite. "My father says I can decide myself. I am thankful to God, because I know most fathers don't allow their daughters to make such decisions. So I have come to ask whether I should marry Pierre."

"You are wise to come to us, Marguerite," said Queen Justice. "Women need to use their minds as well as their hearts in important decisions like marriage."

"How does Pierre treat you?" asked Queen Honesty.

"He is very charming," said Marguerite. "He tells me that I am beautiful, and he writes me poems about love."

"What happens if you disagree with him?" inquired Queen Reason.

Marguerite paused. "Last night we were at a ball. Another man named Albert asked me to dance. He is a childhood friend." She bit her lip. "Pierre got furious when I danced with Albert. He thinks I am too easily influenced by other men."

"What did you say to Pierre?" asked Queen Justice.

"I told him that Albert and I grew up together, and that he is just a friend to me. I told Pierre I was upset he didn't trust me.

"Then he took my hand and said, 'My dearest, I will always know what's best for you! When we are married I will protect you from everyone.'"

Queen Honesty nodded. "I see. Tell me, do you talk with Pierre about things that interest you?" she asked.

Marguerite thought for a moment. "Well, Pierre talks to me about how he goes hunting with other noblemen. I talk to him about my studies of the Bible . . ." She stopped and frowned.

"Are you understanding something?" asked Queen Reason.

"Yes," said Marguerite. "I realize that when Pierre talks to me about hunting, I shudder inside and wonder how he could kill innocent animals. And when I talk to him about the Bible, he pats my hand and changes the subject."

"What is it you like about Pierre?" asked Queen Justice.

"I like his looks. He is tall with black hair and deep blue eyes . . . ." Marguerite hesitated again.

"Yes?" Queen Justice prompted.

"I'm remembering that during the ball, Pierre and I walked by a huge mirror in the hallway. I was thinking that we looked like a handsome couple. But Pierre looked only at himself. He smoothed his hair and smiled, saying, 'Magnificent!'"

The three queens whispered to one another.

"Do you wish to hear our advice, Marguerite?" asked Queen Honesty.

"Yes, please, Queen Honesty," said Marguerite.

"You have explained well the situation between you and Pierre," said the queen. "Indeed, you have begun already to see the truth. You are seeing that underneath Pierre's charm, he is jealous and possessive. This will only increase when you are married. And he will be more critical."

Marguerite nodded sadly in agreement.

"Pierre has been brought up to see women as incapable of thinking," said Queen Reason. "He does not take your Bible study seriously. He seems like many men of our time who insist that women are silly and simple-minded."

"And though he may be handsome," added Queen Honesty, "he seems concerned only for himself. I do not believe him capable of true love."

Queen Reason smiled at Marguerite. "God has blessed men and women with the ability to truly love each other."

"But this kind of love needs much wisdom and understanding," declared Queen Justice. "And we must work to get rid of negative attitudes that cause men to look down on women."

A servant entered the room with a tray of cakes and tea. The queens and Marguerite helped themselves. What a delightful place this is, Marguerite thought.

"Marguerite," said Queen Honesty as she finished her tea, "How would you have answered our questions if Albert were the groom instead of Pierre?"

Marguerite was astonished. "Albert?" she asked. "Albert," she repeated his name more thoughtfully. "Albert enjoys stories I tell him from my Bible reading. It was he who got me interested in the Bible when we were children. We've even prayed together. And Albert never feels jealous when people like me."

"It seems Albert has his heart and mind in the right place," said Queen Reason. "Do the two of you ever argue?"

"Sometimes," smiled Marguerite. "But we quickly get over it. He's not stubborn about his opinions and is open to hearing mine. We laugh a lot, too. I've always thought of Albert as a best friend."

Marguerite looked at the queens with a dawning awareness. "I think I see what you mean. Albert and I are already dear friends. He respects my ideas, and we have many similar interests." She touched her hand to her chest. "I think I just felt my heart flutter!" A radiant smile broke across her face.

"Yes, my dear," responded Queen Justice. "Friendship is the better part of love. Albert seems a very good choice for you to consider marrying if Albert feels the same way."

The three queens prayed with Marguerite for God's guidance in her final decision.

*T*he Paris nobles enjoyed The City of Ladies, *as did many other people who read the book. During her lifetime, Christine's books and poetry were widely read. She was able to support her children while writing about things that were important to her: the rights of women and the need for mutual respect between men and women. Christine spent her last ten years of life in a religious community where her daughter was a nun. After her death, her works remained popular for more than a hundred years.*

Talk about It

- The success of Christine de Pisan was truly remarkable because of attitudes toward women during the time she lived. Why do you think her work was so well received despite those attitudes? How might the church have helped to change attitudes toward women?

- How might you use your writing to bring about good changes for yourself, your family, or your community? Have each family member write down or dictate a short positive message for everyone else in the family. Share them with one another.

Prayer

Dear Lord, bless our family with the gift of expressing ourselves through writing. Let the things we read and write help us become more and more true to ourselves, to the good and kind and honest people you have made us to be. Amen.

The Wonderfully Wacky Water Clock

LEONARDO DA VINCI
1452–1519

eonardo da Vinci (VEEN-chee) must have had a brain without an "off" switch. Consumed with curiosity about the world around him, he carried a notebook everywhere. He drew birds in flight, plants in bloom, weather patterns, and idea after idea for mechanical inventions.

He wrote his notes in a secret code called mirror-writing. All the words were written backward. By holding the notes up to a mirror, they became readable to ordinary mortals. Fascinated by the art of drawing, Leonardo improved his skills by dissecting corpses to better understand the structure of human muscles, veins, and bone formation.

Leonardo was born in the small Italian hill town of Vinci during a period that became known as the Renaissance (ren-uh-SAHNS), a time when there was great interest in art, science, literature, and inventions. Wealthy Italian families like the Medici (MED-uh-chee) princes of Florence supported artists by giving them money to create paintings and sculptures. What a perfect time for Leonardo to express his inventiveness!

Can you imagine what his teenage years were like?

"LEONARDO!" CALLED FRANCESCO (Fran-CHES-koh) from the door of the villa. No answer. "Where is that boy off to now?" he muttered to himself. Peering down the hill toward the small Italian village of Vinci, he saw no sign of the boy.

"We have to leave for the city of Florence right now," Francesco grumbled, stomping into his bedroom to finish packing. "I bet that boy is back at those cliffs I showed him yesterday." He remembered how the birds flying into the wind had caught Leonardo's attention.

Francesco was Leonardo's young uncle. He was also Leonardo's closest companion and his teacher as well. The fifteen-year-old boy responded hungrily to the lessons Francesco prepared. The two of them enjoyed hours of pleasure exploring the countryside.

Leonardo's father was a lawyer who traveled a good deal. He had recently married and moved to the bustling city of Florence. Francesco and Leonardo were to join Leonardo's father and step-mother in their new home.

"But we're not going to get there by nightfall unless Leonardo gets home!" muttered Francesco, throwing the last of his shirts into the packing case. "I can never get that sleepyhead out of bed in the morning, but once he's up, there's no stopping him."

He heard footsteps pounding up the stairs.

"Here I am, Francesco!" laughed a breathless Leonardo, his notebook tightly in hand. "Sorry I'm late. A flock of butterflies swarmed over the cliff and I just had to sketch them."

"Hurry and change into a fresh shirt, Leonardo," interrupted Francesco. "The one you're wearing is covered in mud. We should be on our way already!"

Leonardo darted out of Francesco's room. "I'll be ready," he called back. "And I've figured out an easier way to load the packing cases onto the cart."

Perched on his seat in the horse-drawn cart, Leonardo's eyes grew huge as they passed through the streets of Florence. The city was breathtaking. Pencil flying furiously across his notebook pages, he sketched a graceful clock tower, an arched bridge, and the giant dome of a cathedral.

They entered a town square, or piazza (pee-AHT-suh), decorated with beautiful marble sculptures and surrounded by soft yellow buildings roofed with red tile. The cobblestone streets radiated heat from the warm summer sun.

"The Medici princes contributed most of the funds for the architecture and sculpture you see, Leonardo," said Francesco.

"I want to see the paintings of the great artists, too," said Leonardo eagerly.

"Yes, yes," Francesco nodded. "Your father has arranged for you to meet the master painter and sculptor, Verrocchio (vuh-RAH-kee-oh). If he thinks you have enough talent, he'll invite you to work with him and learn his trade."

Leonardo's brown eyes gleamed. "I'll pray to God that he will make it so!"

Leonardo's father and stepmother warmly greeted the travelers at the door of their new home. They led Francesco and Leonardo upstairs to their bedrooms.

"Oh, a view of the piazza!" exclaimed Leonardo as he looked out the window. "I can sketch from my bedroom, too."

"I'm glad you're happy with your room, Leonardo," his father said. "And I have good news. I've arranged for you to meet Master Verrocchio three days from now."

"Oh, thank you, Father," Leonardo said, hugging him. "Working with Master Verrocchio is my heart's desire."

"There's one small problem," his father added. "The appointment is for five-thirty in the morning. Verrocchio keeps early hours and has strict rules for his apprentices."

Leonardo winced, recalling that he had trouble getting up by ten o'clock, let alone five in the morning. "Francesco can wake me up, Father," he offered.

"No, Leonardo," said his father. "You are responsible for getting yourself to this meeting." He left the room.

Leonardo looked glumly at Francesco. Then his face brightened. "I know. I'll invent a clock that will wake me up."

Early the next morning, Francesco was deep in sleep, exhausted from his long day of travel. As he snored, his feet stuck out from under the linen sheet. Suddenly he felt something cold and wet pouring over his feet. Leaping out of bed, he hollered, "Help! Help! I'm drowning!"

Through sleep-filled eyes, he saw a spindly wooden contraption at the end of his bed. Leonardo stood beside it, doubled over in laughter.

"It works!" Leonardo exclaimed triumphantly. "My water alarm clock works! It woke you up right at the stroke of five!"

"Look, do you see?" asked Leonardo, his finger jabbing the air and pointing toward his invention. "I measured just the right amount of water in the upper container. Then the water slowly trickled into the lower compartment. When it was full—at exactly the right time—the lower compartment opened and poured water onto your feet!"

He glanced at Francesco's angry face. "Hmmmm. But perhaps I have to use something other than water to wake up the person." Leonardo frowned. "I know! I can make a lever that shoves your foot . . ." His voice trailed off as he noticed Francesco's silence.

"I'll change your sheets for you, Francesco," said Leonardo coaxingly. "Don't you like my invention?"

Francesco pointed to the door. "We'll talk more about this later," he sputtered. "Now take this contraption out of here and practice it on yourself."

Two days later, just before five o'clock in the morning, Francesco in bed was sleeping soundly. Suddenly a wooden lever at the end of the bed shot forward and whomped his right foot.

The sleeping figure jerked awake. "Yes!" yelled Leonardo, jumping out of bed and hopping around on his left foot. "Hooray! The lever works!"

He scrambled into his clothes, massaging his sore foot. "I just have to modify the force of the lever's thrust," he muttered, limping down the stairs and off to his interview.

Leonardo arrived at Verrocchio's studio clutching his notebook. Early morning sunlight streamed through the room. Dozens of shelves held marble sculptures in various stages of completion. Leonardo sniffed the pungent smell of linseed oil and grinned. To his right, a young apprentice painted in fluffy clouds as background to a Verrocchio landscape. Another student ground paint pigment with a mortar and pestle. Others stretched canvas over wood panels for future paintings.

Verrocchio walked toward Leonardo wearing a dusty smock and carrying a paint palette covered with blobs of brilliant blues, reds, and yellows. "Good morning, Leonardo," he said.

Leonardo bowed, "Good morning, Master Verrocchio."

"You've brought some of your sketches?"

"Yes, sir," replied Leonardo, handing him the notebook.

Verrocchio put down his paint palette and opened the notebook. He carefully examined each sketch, his face expressionless. "There is raw talent here," he said. "Your interests are varied to be sure. Are you willing to learn how to draw, my boy?"

Leonardo gulped, for he thought he already knew how to draw. Then he straightened his shoulders and declared, "Yes, sir. I want to learn all I can from you."

"Very well," said Verrocchio. "First you will learn the techniques of drawing. Then you will learn to use oil paint, then finally to sculpt. At times, the work will seem long and tiring. But if you are disciplined and ask our Creator for his divine guidance, your creativity will bloom."

"Thank you, Master Verrocchio. God has answered my heart's desire."

"By the way," Verrocchio asked, pointing to a drawing in Leonardo's notebook, "does this alarm clock contraption actually work?"

Leonardo da Vinci worked hard as Verrocchio's apprentice, eventually outshining him. In his adult years, Leonardo painted the most famous painting in the world, The Mona Lisa—the lady with the mysterious smile. Perhaps his greatest achievement was The Last Supper. In this painting, Leonardo used his God-given creativity to show Jesus and his disciples gathered at a final meal the evening before Jesus was crucified.

Leonardo da Vinci symbolizes the best of God's talents in all of us. He was an artist and scientist and inventor of extraordinary ability and interest. Even today, Leonardo's work is held in the greatest respect. The notebooks filled with his mirror-writing and sketches are prized and studied by scholars throughout the world.

Talk about It

- Like Leonardo, each of us has some special abilities from God—abilities that can make a wonderful difference to others. What hobbies and talents do each of you possess? How might these gifts be used in serving the Lord?

- Leonardo was a perfectionist. He was never satisfied with his work. He had difficulty completing projects because he could always see ways to improve them. What are the advantages and disadvantages of being a perfectionist? What advice would you have given Leonardo?

Prayer

Lord, please bring out the creativity within each of us so that we can enjoy our individual gifts and talents. Guide our family to develop the delicate balance between creativity, discipline, and responsibility to others.

The Morning Star of Wittenberg

KATHERINE VON BORA
1499–1552

*I*n the early 1500s, German reformer Martin Luther challenged what he felt were corrupt beliefs and practices in the church. Luther believed people were made right with God through faith in Jesus, not by buying pardon from priests. Some church leaders were upset and expelled Luther from the church. The Catholic emperor declared him an outlaw.

Katherine von Bora was one of many nuns who agreed with Luther. Katherine decided to leave her convent. She and several other nuns hid in a cart and escaped to the town of Wittenberg, Germany.

Martin heard of their daring getaway. He knew these brave women were now without support. So Luther helped arrange marriages for the ex-nuns. Katherine, however, refused to marry the man chosen for her.

Two years later, Katherine met Martin Luther. The former priest was impressed by her devout faith, good humor, and practical intelligence. He asked her to marry him, and she accepted. As was common for the time, their marriage began as an act of mutual convenience. But could this union blossom into love?

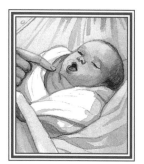

KATHERINE QUIETLY SLID OUT OF BED, careful not to disturb Martin. It was only four o'clock and still dark outside. She knelt on the wooden floor by her bed and began her morning prayers.

For a long time she knelt. At last she stood and smiled down on Martin; he was snoring peacefully. She changed out of her nightgown and wound her dark brown hair into a twist, covering it with a white cap. Then she tied on an apron and headed down three flights of stairs to the large kitchen.

The Luthers had been given this three-story building as a wedding gift from a wealthy German noble who supported Martin's ideas. Formerly a dormitory, the home was located near the great University of Wittenberg.

"This is a perfect place for us," said Katherine to herself as she stoked up the fire in the large brick oven. "It's big—really too big for Martin and me. But for now it helps serve visitors and students from the university who need lodging." She mixed bread dough and kneaded it into long, slender loaves.

"Soon we'll be needing some of the bedrooms for the children God gives us," she mused, happily patting her protruding stomach. "And the first one will arrive any day now!"

Measuring out flour, she began to mix biscuits for breakfast. She said to herself. "I'll ask the cook to make sausages and eggs, too. That should be enough to feed everyone."

Several theologians and noblemen had arrived the night before to talk with Martin. Katherine looked forward to lively conversation at breakfast.

Morning sunlight poured through the leaded windows of the dining hall. Platters of steaming sausages and hot biscuits were passed by student helpers. The long refectory table grew animated with conversation and laughter as the Luthers' guests filled their plates. Sitting at the head of the table, Martin spoke intensely with guests on either side of him. Katherine sat at the other end, flanked by two visiting theologians. She looked forward to using her Latin again in conversation with these guests. She noticed that her husband's plate was full, but he hadn't yet touched his breakfast. *The only thing Martin loves more than good food is good conversation*, she thought.

Just then Martin looked up and caught Katherine's eye. He winked appreciatively. Good conversation, good breakfast—an altogether good morning.

A messenger appeared at the door of the hall. He held up an official-looking scroll as he scanned the diners. Katherine nodded to him, and the man brought her the note then quickly left. She broke the wax seal and felt her heart stop as she read the message: "Beware, Luther's life is in danger. The emperor has sent someone to poison him." There was no signature.

"Dear God, no!" Katherine gasped. She sent a student to look for the messenger, but he had vanished.

Quickly she summoned two servers. One young man quickly removed Martin's breakfast plate to the kitchen. Another young man replaced it with Katherine's breakfast.

Martin glanced at her curiously, but he was too absorbed in his discussion to take much note. He absently-mindedly finished Katherine's breakfast.

Katherine excused herself from the table and hurried to the kitchen. "We must test all food placed in front of Doctor Luther," she said to the cook.

The cook was one step ahead of her, having been informed by the server. She'd found a mouse to whom she was feeding bits of the breakfast, so far with no ill effects.

"Only you and I will prepare and serve the doctor's meals until this threat is over," said Katherine.

Later, when they were alone in Martin's study, Katherine gave him the note.

"So that is why you exchanged my breakfast," said Martin soberly. "What a clever, good-hearted woman you are, Katherine. You take good care of me."

"I am very worried for you, my dear," said Katherine.

Martin patted her hand. "With you and God at my side, I shall be safe. I'll make immediate inquiries into this threat."

Early the next morning, Katherine sat with a fishing pole by the pond behind their house. Graceful willows lined the shore, and ducks paddled through the still green water.

She was pulling in her sixth trout when she saw Martin walking toward her. "Good morning, my doctor!" she said.

Martin smiled and sat down beside her. "Ah, the pond is beautiful in the morning. And I see the fish are cooperating! I have good news," he added.

Katherine forgot the fishing. "About the note?" she asked.

"Yes. It was reported to me just now that they found the messenger who brought it. He confessed to writing it himself." Martin frowned. "He wanted to frighten us, to stop my work."

"Is he acting on his own?" asked Katherine anxiously.

"That is what he says."

"I pray that he's telling the truth," said Katherine. "But nothing will stop us from obeying the Lord."

She got up and laughed, looking at all the fish. "Now if you'll help carry these creatures, I'll cook a breakfast feast."

That night Katherine nibbled at her food. Just to be on the safe side, she and the cook had prepared and served Martin's dinner. But something else was bothering Katherine. All afternoon abdominal cramps had distracted her.

A sudden sharp pain took her breath away. Clutching her stomach, she realized that the baby was on its way.

Martin got up and hurried to her.

"It's started, Martin," Katherine whispered to him. "The baby is coming."

Luther turned to their guests. "Excuse us, gentlemen. God willing, we are about to be blessed with a child." Martin carefully guided Katherine out of the dining hall.

"Johann," Katherine called to one of the student helpers, "find the midwife and bring her straight to our room."

At midnight the midwife came out of the Luthers' bedroom. Martin had been pacing up and down the hallway.

"I can stay with you only a moment, Doctor Luther," she said. "I've rarely seen a woman so brave. Mrs. Luther refuses to cry out in pain. She prays and takes deep breaths and worries about you. She asked me to tell you that she is fine and the baby will be here soon."

Martin shook his head in wonder. "That sounds like the Katherine I know and love . . ." He stopped pacing. "I just spoke the word 'love.' Can it be that I not only admire Katherine, but I've fallen in love with her?"

An hour later, Martin heard cries of a newborn baby. The midwife opened the bedroom door, and Martin dashed over to his wife.

Comfortably propped against big pillows lay a tired but radiant Katherine. The baby was in her arms, wrapped in soft linen.

"Oh, Martin," cried Katherine, "God has blessed us with a son!"

"God be praised," rejoiced Martin, reaching out to stroke his son's cheek.

Katherine lifted the baby into Martin's waiting arms.

"My dearest Katherine," said Martin, rocking the baby in his arms, "my new family is a true miracle of the Lord's grace." He looked upward with moist eyes. "And I give you thanks, Jesus, my Savior!"

Looking tenderly at Katherine, he asked, "Shall we name him 'Hans,' after your father?"

"Oh, Martin! My father would be so pleased," she beamed.

Martin placed little Hans in her arms and kissed her gently. "Today I found out how deeply I love you, my dear. You are my Katie, my morning star of Wittenberg!"

*K*atie and Martin had six children. They quickly filled their large home with their own children plus many of Martin's nephews and nieces, the orphaned children of friends, and some of Katie's relatives. Add to that an assortment of tutors, student boarders, and visitors from afar, and you can see how much Katie's good cheer and administrative abilities helped Martin Luther. Skilled in health care, Katie was able to cure Martin's frequent illnesses as well as lifting his often flagging spirits. Her intelligence, education, and training as a nun equipped Katie to be a vital sounding board and source of ideas as Martin struggled with issues of theology and church politics. And the love that matured between Martin and Katie transformed their home into a powerful expression of God's grace and a firm base for the Protestant Reformation.

Talk about It

- Why do you think Martin fell in love with Katie?

- In the last book of the Bible, Revelation 22:16, Jesus says, "I am . . . the Bright Morning Star." What did Martin find in Katie that reminded him of Jesus, that made her his "morning star of Wittenberg"?

- We have choices to make about how we react to daily family crises. When we respond with courage and good cheer instead of grumpiness or grudging cooperation, what happens to those around us?

Prayer

Lord, please bring good cheer into the heart of our family. Reveal ways for us to show our caring and humor. When we feel cranky, help us talk with you about it so that we can lift each other's spirits with our own courage, love, and laughter.

Woman Preacher on Trial

ANNE HUTCHINSON
1592–1637

I n the 1600s, many people sailed from England to North America in order to worship God as they wished. Some of these people felt the Church of England had become too concerned about worship practices and had forgotten the Bible. They wanted to purify the church. So they became known as Puritans. Puritans stressed godly living, simple worship, plain clothing, and churches without decoration.

A group of Puritans settled in the Massachusetts Bay Colony near what is now Boston. Then a serious problem erupted. The Puritans started arguing among themselves over religious views. Governor John Winthrop thought this problem was caused by the influence of one woman—Anne Hutchinson.

Anne led a women's prayer group that taught that every person should be able to decide for himself or herself what to believe about God. Her followers also argued that the church should not be involved in business and politics. Anne and her followers often got in trouble with authorities in church and government.

ANNE WRAPPED THE NEWBORN BABY snugly in a clean cloth and handed him to his mother. "Here, Frances," Anne said softly. "God has blessed you with a wonderful boy."

"Oh, Anne, he's beautiful," cried Frances, cuddling the baby in her arms. "Thanks for your skill in delivering him."

Anne smiled down at the young woman. "I'll get his father," she said. "I imagine he'd like to hold his firstborn son."

Anne walked home exhausted but happy. It had been an all-night delivery. The next morning Anne held a Bible as she taught the prayer group assembled in her home. A fire blazed in the hearth, and candles shed a soft light on the earnest faces. Sixty people, mostly women, crowded in to hear her.

"The Reverend Cotton preached on Sunday about how God saves us by his grace, not by any efforts we make to be saved," Anne explained. "To me, this is a very important idea. For one thing, it means that when Jesus died, he wiped away our sins for us. We are truly forgiven."

Several women nodded. "Tell us more about grace," one asked.

"Grace is God's gift to you—because he loves you. It's a very personal thing between God and you," Anne said. "When God saves you, his Spirit lives within you to help you believe and to guide your behavior."

"Does that mean we don't need the church's laws to guide us?" asked another woman.

Anne hesitated before answering. This was the issue that often got her and her followers in trouble. "It means you should be primarily guided by God," she replied firmly.

After the meeting, everyone helped themselves to cakes and hot cider. Even though spring was early this year, there would be a chill in the morning air as they walked home.

Anne's husband, William, walked outside with the last of the group. When he returned, he smiled at Anne said, "That was a stimulating meeting."

Anne looked up and nodded. "Yes, the group seems very interested in our talks."

"I hope there are no more complaints about the prayer meetings," William said. "One man today told me he thought you went too far with your words about grace."

Anne sighed. "I'm not saying anything that the Rev. Cotton hasn't preached," she responded. "I think I have the right and the calling from the Lord to teach as I do. So many women tell me how much these meetings encourage them."

"I know," said William. "I see the numbers increase every week. But you know the risk you're taking, my dear. Governor Winthrop and the judges could banish you if they can prove you are threatening the peace of the colony."

"We moved here from England to gain religious freedom," Anne said. "How can I give up what I believe?" She looked at her husband. "Do you think I should stop, William?"

"I think God is with you," he answered. "And I support you, even to the point of moving again if we have to."

Several months later, Anne paced the floor of her kitchen. The smell of cornbread drifted from the oven. Wiping flour-covered hands on her apron, she knelt down on the wooden floor.

"Oh, Lord," she prayed, "you are my guide in all things. Send your Spirit to inspire my words at my trial tomorrow. Help the judges and pastors to understand that my intent is not to harm the colony, but to bring people closer to you."

Anne's thoughts drifted back to her childhood. Her father had been a minister who believed in freedom of worship. He had encouraged her to study the Bible and to learn from his books and sermons. Anne grew up accustomed to speaking her mind.

The Puritans were not allowed to worship freely in England, where she was born. When she and William married, they decided to move to the new colony of Massachusetts to enjoy freedom of religion. Now it looked as if that freedom might be taken from them.

Her thoughts were interrupted by shouts outside. Anne opened the door to see four of her children standing there with pails of maple syrup. "We finished boiling down the syrup," grinned ten-year-old Chastity. "Can we have some for supper?"

"Yes, children," Anne said, hugging each of them. "We'll pour it on the cornbread. Put it by the stove. Supper will be ready soon."

The family gathered around the table while William said grace. Then, as the children ate hungrily, Anne looked at the cozy kitchen, at their comfortable home. "What will happen if we have to move? How can we leave all this?"

The next morning, Anne walked into the church that was used as a courthouse. She wore a gray cotton gown and white cap, for Puritans were required to wear simple unadorned clothing. Anne agreed with this principle. When she had lived in England, Anne thought that too many people were more concerned with their clothing than with their relationship to God.

The church was cold. And it was filled with Puritan men wearing black. Governor Winthrop sat at the front, and two judges sat beside him. Everyone else sat in rows facing them.

Anne was ushered in to stand before the governor and the judges. She shivered as she waited for the trial to begin.

A group of Puritan women from Anne's prayer meeting had assembled quietly in the back.

Governor Winthrop stared at Anne. Then he cleared his throat and spoke: "Anne Hutchinson, you know the charges brought against you. The Massachusetts Bay Colony accuses you of planting seeds of dissatisfaction and disobedience among the people." He leaned toward Anne. "And it accuses you of behaving in a manner unbecoming to a woman. How do you respond, Mrs. Hutchinson?"

Anne did not flinch. She steadily returned his stare. "Governor Winthrop," she asked, "how is it that the colony thinks I have behaved in a manner unbecoming to a woman?"

"Women should stay at home and be good mothers, minding children, cooking and washing; they should care for the cows and chickens and help in the fields. By holding prayer meetings in your home, you have taken on responsibilities not fitting for women."

"Where does the Bible say this is not permitted?" Anne asked.

Governor Winthrop sputtered then said, "The apostle Paul says in 1 Corinthians 14:34 that 'women should be silent in the churches. For they are not permitted to speak, but should be subordinate, as the law also says.'"

Anne replied, "Paul also says in Galatians 3:28, 'There is no longer Jew or Greek, there is no longer slave or free, there is no longer male and female; for all of you are one in Christ Jesus.'"

Governor Winthrop's face grew red. "But you are still required not to speak in churches."

"Nor have I," replied Anne. "Only at home, and the Bible gives us permission to do so. Paul says in Titus 2:3, 'tell the older women to be reverent in behavior . . . they are to teach what is good.'"

The governor did not respond. He scowled at Anne. He had not expected her to use the Bible in her own defense.

Hours of testimony from preachers and judges followed Anne's defense of herself. Finally, it was time for the judges to make their decision. While they discussed her fate, Anne waited outside with William.

"I think their hearts are closed to me, William," said Anne.

An hour later, Anne was called to stand before the judges and Governor Winthrop. William listened by the door. The women from Anne's prayer meetings watched from the back of the church.

"It is our decision," pronounced Governor Winthrop, "that you, Mrs. Hutchinson, are misusing your role as a woman by leading people away from proper doctrine. Therefore, you are hereby banished from the Massachusetts Bay Colony forever."

Shocked gasps erupted from the women at the rear. Silence filled the courtroom as the governor sat down.

Anne stood quietly, her eyes gazing off in the distance. She folded her hands in front of her and bowed her head for a moment. Then she slowly walked to the door to join William. As Anne left, the women who had been inspired by her teaching followed her out the door.

*I*n the spring of 1638, Anne Hutchinson moved with her family to a colony that later became the state of Rhode Island. Here they enjoyed an atmosphere more open to religious differences. William died a few years later, and Anne was killed by Native Americans in 1643. Today Anne Hutchinson receives the respect she is due as one of the earliest woman preachers and the first defender of religious freedom in New England.

Talk about It

- Anne defended herself by using the Bible, but so did Governor Winthrop. Who do you think won the argument? What do you think was the real reason why Anne was banished from the colony?

- Do you feel that there is religious freedom in your country? In your church? What religious beliefs divide Christians today? How do you think these can be resolved?

Prayer

Thank you, Heavenly Father, for showing us through your son Jesus that we are truly loved and that we are saved by grace. Help us to respect different ways of worshiping and to love others as we love ourselves.

The *Lily* of the Mohawks

KATERI TEKAKWITHA
1656–1680

*T*he arrival of Europeans brought major changes to the New World. Tribes like the Mohawk, Iroquois (IHR-uh-kwoy), and Algonquin (al-GAHN-kwun) alternated times of peace and trading with times of fighting the newcomers.

Kateri (kuh-TER-ee) Tekakwitha (Tuh-KAK-with-uh) was born in a small Mohawk village in what is now upstate New York. Her father was a chief; her mother was among the earliest converts to Christianity. Sadly, both her parents died of smallpox when Kateri was only four.

Mohawk homes were long wooden buildings that housed several families. The women prepared meals together and the men hunted in groups. At times life could be frightening. At any moment, a rival tribe could attack and steal away prisoners.

Into this world came the blackrobes, French Catholic priests who brought Christianity. They were called blackrobes because they wore long woolen black robes with silver crosses hanging around their waists.

It took great courage for any Native American to convert to Christianity. Such individuals were often persecuted by their tribe for betraying the tribal heritage and selling out to the Europeans.

KATERI SAT CROSS-LEGGED ON THE FLOOR of the Mohawk longhouse sewing tiny blue and white beads on a soft doeskin tunic. Smoke from the fire stung her eyes. *My eyes are still weak from the smallpox,* she thought. Her fingers rubbed her cheek, where she felt the roughness of smallpox scars.

I am grateful to be alive, she thought, sadly remembering how her parents had died of the dreaded disease brought by the white men. She now lived with her uncle and aunt. Her uncle was a chief, as Kateri's father had been. Bitter toward the white men, her uncle especially hated the blackrobes.

But Kateri didn't hate the blackrobes. She felt curious about them, for these men with silver crosses had taught her mother the way of Christianity. Kateri wanted to know more about the God of the blackrobes—the God who had made her mother so happy. But how could she learn? Her uncle and aunt had forbidden her to go near the blackrobes' chapel.

"How can I learn to speak to the blackrobes' God?" whispered Kateri as she embroidered the tunic. "Rowanniio (roh-WAHN-ee-oh) is the name my people give to the God of the blackrobes." Repeating the name Rowanniio several times under her breath, Kateri smiled to herself.

"What are you whispering about?" asked her aunt abruptly.

Kateri looked up to see her Aunt Arosen (ah-ROH-sun) leaning over her.

"You know your uncle has forbidden anyone in his house to mention Rowanniio. Now quiet your tongue and help me with the corn cakes for our meal."

Meekly laying down her sewing, Kateri stood up. "I will gladly help you, Aunt," she replied softly.

The next morning, Kateri prepared food for the noon meal. She took the extra food to the elderly of the village. That afternoon she sewed intricate patterns of beadwork onto a headband. Many in the tribe admired Kateri's beadwork. Before dinnertime Kateri spent an hour with the others in the fields, planting and weeding the crops.

Yet none of this activity filled the empty hole inside her.

The more she thought about it, the more Kateri felt convinced that the Christian God could make her feel complete. Her mother had told her before she died that peace and joy came through the one true God, Rowanniio.

Trudging home from the fields, Kateri decided she would ask the blackrobes' God for help. So Kateri said her first prayer. "Rowanniio," she breathed, "please help me to become a Christian."

Rounding a corner to her uncle's longhouse, Kateri noticed a blackrobe standing at the door of a nearby dwelling. He was talking to her friend Anatasia (ah-nuh-TAH-zhuh) and her family. He paused to smile at Kateri.

Kateri peeked inside her longhouse and saw that no one was back from the fields. Kateri decided to risk punishment. She joined Anatasia's family and the blackrobe.

The priest welcomed her. "God be with you, my child," he said. "I am Father de Lambertville (duh-LAM-ber-veel)."

Kateri blushed red as scarlet. "Hello, Father."

"Your friend Anatasia tells me your uncle disapproves of the blackrobes," he said.

"Yes, that is true. But I want to become a Christian even so," Kateri said, surprised at the determination in her voice.

"Even if you are punished because of it, my child?" asked Father de Lambertville in a serious tone.

"Yes. My mother was a Christian, and I, too, want to know Rowanniio," she blurted out, tears in her eyes.

"Come tomorrow to the chapel. I will baptize you and then give you instruction," he replied.

As Father de Lambertville walked away, Kateri felt an enormous sense of joy. *Is this how my mother felt?* she wondered. "Thank you, Rowanniio," she prayed.

Minutes later her uncle's family returned from the fields.

"Where is our meal, Kateri?" asked her aunt. "We are hungry from the day's work."

"I am sorry, Aunt Arosen," Kateri replied. "It will be ready soon." She eyed her uncle as she stirred the stew pot. Kateri knew that tonight she would have to tell him about Father de Lambertville. She could not hide such a thing from him.

Later Kateri saw her uncle sitting alone by the longhouse fire smoking his pipe. She decided that now was the time to tell him. "Please help me, Rowanniio," she prayed.

"Uncle," Kateri said, her voice wavering, "may I talk with you about something?"

He glanced up at her and nodded, gesturing for her to sit.

Kateri knelt on the thick beaver pelts near him. "Uncle, you know I have always been obedient," she began.

"That is so," he replied, eyeing her suspiciously.

She looked down at her trembling hands. "Oh, give me strength," she prayed silently. Out of nowhere a sense of confidence filled her. She straightened up and lifted her head, gazing with steadfast eyes at her uncle.

"I have a great longing in my heart to become a Christian like my mother was. I have made a decision to be baptized tomorrow by Father de Lambertville."

Her uncle threw down his pipe. "You say you are obedient? I forbade my family to speak with the blackrobes." He shook his head in disgust. "You are a disgrace to the Mohawk tribe!"

Kateri drew a breath and let it out slowly. "My mother was a Mohawk and my father allowed her to become a Christian," she replied respectfully. "I must be obedient to what my heart tells me to do."

"I will not stop you," snarled her uncle. "But neither will I stop the women in my family from punishing you for your decision." He got up and walked out of the longhouse.

Early the next morning Kateri dressed in her beaded tunic. She wanted to look her best for her baptism. She wondered if her friend Anatasia would be baptized at the same time. Kateri knew that Anatasia's family would feel happy about their daughter's conversion.

Yet despite her excitement, Kateri felt tired. Her aunt had been furious about Kateri's decision and had made her clean the longhouse during the night while the others slept. "I am about to become a Christian and that is all that matters," Kateri told herself.

She crept out of the longhouse so as not to waken anyone and then ran down the path to the small wooden chapel. Surrounded by a stand of silver birch trees, the chapel welcomed her with its door open wide. She entered and saw Anatasia talking to Father de Lambertville.

"You're here!" exclaimed her friend, running up to hug Kateri. "I was hoping we could be baptized together!"

From in front of the altar, Father de Lambertville beckoned the two girls forward.

As Kateri walked up the short aisle, she noticed that little niches in the chapel walls held bouquets of fragrant white lilies. As Father de Lambertville explained about the baptism ceremony, Kateri heard the creek through the open window and felt the breeze that rustled the silver birch trees.

Father de Lambertville brought out the water and baptized Anatasia while Kateri watched.

Then Kateri stood with her hands folded while Father de Lambertville poured the water on her head. Above the sound of the creek and the rustle of the trees, his voice rang out: "I baptize you, Kateri Tekakwitha, in the name of the Father, and of the Son, and of the Holy Spirit. Amen." He smiled at Kateri. "You are now a child of Rowanniio."

Peace and joy flooded Kateri's soul. "I hope I am worthy of his love," she whispered.

Father de Lambertville took two lilies from the walls of the chapel and handed them to the girls. "You are God's little flower. You are his lily of the Mohawks," he said to Kateri.

Although Kateri experienced abuse from her Mohawk tribe, she never wavered in her decision to put God first in her life. She lived a gentle, obedient life in the Lord. Later she found her way to a Christian village away from the abuse in her tribe. The priests became concerned when Kateri began to punish herself by fasting and going without sleep for periods of time. Perhaps she believed that Christians were supposed to suffer for their faith; or perhaps it was because she had gotten used to the cruelty and abuse of her family.

When Kateri died at twenty-four, she was greatly loved by everyone in the village for her unselfish devotion to others. At the moment of her death, it is said that the smallpox scars on her face vanished and she glowed with beauty. Her gravestone reads: "Kateri Tekakwitha, the most beautiful flower that bloomed among the Indians."

Talk about It

- God answered Kateri's secret prayers to help her get to know him better and to become a Christian. Are there any secret prayers you have said to God that he later fulfilled?

- Like Kateri, we, too, often feel we aren't good or perfect enough. And it's hard to realize that God loves and accepts us as we are. Why do you think Kateri felt she deserved to be punished? If she was your friend, how would you help her better understand God's love?

Prayer

Dear God, you alone can fill the empty place in our hearts. Help us understand how much you love us, so we can relax and love you back. Amen.

Joy at Work

JOHANN SEBASTIAN BACH
1685–1750

hy is Johann (YOH-hahn) Sebastian (suh-BASS-chun) Bach (BAHK) often called the fifth evangelist? He wasn't a preacher. He didn't write any of the Bible. But his musical contributions rank him alongside Matthew, Mark, Luke, and John in spreading the story of Jesus.

Today Bach's St. Matthew Passion *and* St. John Passion *are performed every Easter throughout the world, bringing the good news about Jesus to millions of people. You also can hear Bach's hymn music in churches around the world.*

But in spite of his burning desire to write music for God's glory, Bach's life wasn't easy. He was never appreciated during his time as organist and choirmaster at St. Thomas Church in Leipzig, Germany. He was paid so poorly that he could hardly support his large family. And although he was famous as a great organist while he lived, it wasn't until the 1800s that his music compositions were appreciated.

Indeed, Bach's earthly life could have been pretty grim if it hadn't been for his loving family.

BACH DIPPED HIS PEN into the ink pot, gently shook off the excess ink, and jotted down notes of the music floating in his head. Candlelight shone on the manuscript paper. Clusters of black notes poured onto the page as Bach hurried to complete the first part of his latest composition.

He heard the grandfather clock chime twice. *Two A.M.,* he thought. *Have I been at this since ten this morning?* He smiled then said, "Thank you, Lord, for helping me. It is your music I am writing." Bach stood up, stretched his arms, and yawned.

"I have to be up in four hours to rehearse the choirboys," he sighed. Bach peered out the window into the spring night. Next door, the graceful spires of St. Thomas Church were dark silhouettes against a moonlit sky. *The new pastor wants me to teach even more classes,* he thought. *How can I find the time to write the Lord's music?*

He returned to his desk and eyed the manuscript he'd been working on. Seeing that the ink had dried, he tenderly placed the half-completed composition on a shelf. *I'll try to get back to this tomorrow,* he thought. Bach picked up the candlestick from his desk and headed up the stairs to bed.

On his way, he peeked into the children's bedrooms and saw that all eight were peacefully sleeping, two in a bed. One of little Wilhelm's legs stuck out of the covers. Bach tucked it under the feather comforter and caressed the boy's cheek.

Entering his bedroom, Bach paused to look at his wife as she slept. Anna Magdalena's long dark hair curled around her shoulders and fanned out into a soft halo around her face. Sliding into bed carefully, Bach dozed off within moments.

At eight o'clock the next morning, Anna and the children were finishing breakfast when Johann dragged in from the choirboy rehearsal. The children and Anna chattered noisily, passing pitchers of milk, platters of sliced cheese, and freshly baked brown bread.

"Good morning, dear Johann," greeted Anna.

Bach slid into his chair at the head of the table.

"How did rehearsal go?" Anna asked.

"Awful. Many of the boys don't want to sing," he replied with a scowl. "They lack discipline and act up during practice." He took a slice of cheese. "One piece of good news is that I am about to interview someone to teach the Latin class. That way I can devote more time to my composing."

"That sounds promising," smiled Anna.

Bach gazed around the table at his children and his scowl melted. "And as for you, dear children, would you like me to play the harpsichord this morning during our music practice?"

"Oh, yes, Papa!" the children chorused.

"Would you play the song you wrote just for us?" piped up little Wilhelm.

"Yes, my son," Bach laughed. "I will do that."

After breakfast, they gathered in the large room Bach had set aside for their practices. The room had four windows that looked out onto the flowers of a nearby meadow. Musical instruments were scattered everywhere in the cheerful three-story house, but most of them were here in the practice room. A harpsichord and a clavichord, which looked like small pianos, faced each other by one of the windows. Violins and a cello lay against chairs. Little notebooks with musical exercises written by Bach were stacked on the harpsichord.

Anna Magdalena was an accomplished singer, but Bach was teaching her and the children to play keyboard instruments.

"Come, children. Come, Anna," invited Bach. "At Wilhelm's request, let me play and sing the little song I wrote for you."

They surrounded the harpsichord, and Bach's fingers picked out a lilting, lively tune on the keys. When he finished, Bach stood and took a dramatic bow while Anna and the children clapped wildly.

The music lessons were well underway when there was a knock at the front door. Bach left everyone to their playing and singing and went to the door.

There stood the pastor of St. Thomas Church, the man who had hired Bach. He was frowning. "I need a word with you, Herr Bach," he said. "I will not disturb your family; I can hear that they are busily occupied. Will you come with me to my office for a short while?"

Bach returned the frown, saying, "We are in the midst of music lessons. But if you will give me just a moment, Herr Pastor . . ." He returned to the practice room to excuse himself then followed the pastor to the church office.

Bach sat in a chair opposite the pastor's desk. "It has come to my attention that you plan to hire a substitute to take your place teaching the Latin class. Is this true, Herr Bach?"

"Yes, that is so."

"I fail to see the need for such a step. You were hired, Herr Bach, to teach the boys both music and Latin."

"Yes, Herr Pastor," Bach replied. "But I am creating music for God's glory here at St. Thomas. To do that, I need time for composition. Hiring a substitute for one Latin class gives me a little more of the time I need."

"You have been hired to play music, to direct the choir, and to teach. You have not been hired to compose music," protested the pastor.

"I am writing new music especially for our Lutheran church services," explained Bach. "Until now there has been no music written especially for our churches. I do it not for myself, but for the glory of God, Herr Pastor."

The pastor sighed. He could see that he was getting nowhere with this stubborn musician. "Very well then," he said after a moment. "I will allow you to hire this substitute teacher for the

Latin class—but only for five of the ten weeks you teach it. And you must pay the man out of your salary."

Bach started to argue but thought better of it. "As you wish, Herr Pastor."

Slowly walking back to his home, Bach muttered to himself: "What will I tell Anna Magdalena? We're already on a tight budget. I had to fight just to be allowed to live in this house. I had to argue for every small salary increase I've gotten from this church. I spend half my time arguing, and there's hardly any left to do my work for the Lord."

The sounds of harpsichord, singing, and stringed instruments warmed Bach's heart as he entered the house. He stood just inside the door and listened. From her seat at the harpsichord, Anna saw the gloomy look on her husband's face and quickly went to him.

"Let's go into your study, Johann," she suggested. "The children can continue on their own." Then she and Bach walked into his study and he told her what the pastor had said.

"I sometimes wonder if I shouldn't just give up my composing," sighed Bach. "It would make my life much easier, and yours too, my dear."

"Oh, Johann," said Anna. "You'd be impossible to live with if you didn't write your music! It is everything to you. You must not think of giving it up. Besides, I have good news."

Bach looked at Anna's bright eyes. "You have good news, do you? Well, I could use good news. Tell me!"

"I've been asked to sing at a concert for the duke, in honor of his new duchess," she said. "And he will pay me more than enough to pay for your substitute Latin teacher."

Bach hugged her. "You are such a treasure, Anna Magdalena! I thank God for your understanding and support." He paused then got up and walked to his desk. He was once again hearing beautiful music in his head. Eyeing the manuscript he had been working on the night before, he said, "You know, I think I've got the next part of this music."

Anna laughed as she watched her husband bend over the paper. "I'm sure you do, Johann, I'm sure you do. God be with you, my darling. I'll call you in a few hours when it's time for the next rehearsal with the choirboys."

Bach dipped his pen into the ink pot and joyfully began writing the next passage of his music—for the glory of God.

It was at St. Thomas Church that Bach wrote his music for the Lutheran service, fulfilling a lifelong dream to make music a built-in part of worshiping God in Lutheran church services. Every detail of the liturgy was provided with fitting music. He even wrote chorale preludes for the children's service.

The impact of Bach's music is much stronger today than when he was living. The Voyager *spacecraft, launched in 1977, is carrying a recording deep into outer space. The recording is cast from copper and gold so it will last many, many years. Bach's* Brandenburg Concerto No. 2 *is the first piece of music on the recording. If the spacecraft meets alien life forms, they will hear a composition penned long ago in Bach's study.*

Talk about It

- Bach drew joy from his family life to lift his spirits. How can your family members encourage one another to joy and excellence in pursuing their own interests and talents?

- Listen to part of a recording of Bach's "St. Matthew Passion" or "St. John Passion" with your family. Afterwards, share your reactions. How does Bach's music show you he was influenced by God? Why do you think his work is so well received today?

Prayer

May the joy of the Lord inspire our daily life at home, at school, and at work. We ask you, Creator God, to help us fulfill the purposes you have given us on earth. Amen.

The Storm that Saved a Life

JOHN NEWTON
1725–1807

 orn in England, John Newton spent much of his life ignoring God. His mother died when he was six years old. A religious woman, she had helped him memorize parts of the Bible by the time he was four. But when she died, John lost enthusiasm for anything Christian.

As a commander on a trading ship, John's father was away from home for long periods of time. The young boy was sent to a strict boarding school, where he grew rebellious and sullen. When John was eleven, his father took him along to sea.

For many years young Newton worked in the slave trade, transporting African men, women, and children to other parts of the world, where they were treated with unspeakable cruelty.

In the late 1700s, a Christian revival swept England. A Methodist minister named John Wesley preached about God's love to thousands of people who flocked to hear him. Another powerful speaker, William Wilberforce, spoke out against the evils of slavery.

But the words of these men did not reach the ship on which John Newton sailed. And so God used another way of speaking.

JOHN TRUDGED DOWN THE STAIRS of the ship's hold lugging a heavy bucket of water. "Why can't one of the other sailors do this?" he complained. "This is the sixth time the captain has ordered me down here."

Half the water slopped out of the bucket when he thumped it down in front of the padlocked door. Fumbling for the key, he heard moans and cries from within.

John shoved open the door and peered into the dark. "Here's some water," he said roughly, trying to ignore the foul stench.

The black men inside shuffled clumsily forward, their legs and wrists in chains. John tossed one of them a tin cup, then turned and left, locking the door after him.

"They're just animals, not people," he mumbled to himself as he climbed back to the deck. He breathed in the fresh air of the open sea. The vessel dipped to meet a swelling wave, which sprayed salt water over the deck. The sails billowed in an increasingly gusty wind.

Purple clouds were forming on the horizon of the deep blue Atlantic. The sun was setting. The slave ship was ten days off the coast of Africa, carrying its cargo of men and women west to be sold in the New World.

John had helped to capture the Africans and then assigned each a number in place of their names, which no one bothered to learn. Later he had helped his shipmates chain the slaves in the ship's hold to make sure there was no trouble.

"Did you take the water to the slaves, sailor?" shouted the captain from the ship's helm. He was eyeing John fiercely.

John scowled but answered courteously "Aye, aye, Captain." He didn't want to be given bread and water again for rudeness.

"We're in for rough seas tonight," said the captain, surveying the dark clouds building up in the northern sky. "Go below and tell the first mate I want to see him, sailor. And I want you on night watch."

The deck rolled under John's feet as he made his way down to the crew's quarters. He was tired and hungry, and he was fed up with being ordered around.

Sailors were eating their supper when John walked in. The first mate was telling a story.

"The captain wants you," John interrupted him sourly. "You'll have to save your story."

"I see you're in your usual mood, John," grinned the first mate as he got up to leave.

"The captain's been on my back ever since we started this god-forsaken voyage. I get all the worst jobs. Now he wants me to do night watch, too."

"No wonder the captain's on your back," retorted the first mate. "You never have a good word for anyone—not even him. You'd better watch yourself or you'll be in leg irons like the miserable wretches down in the hold."

John glared at the first mate. "You're acting pretty high and mighty, mister. And those are just animals down there, nothing more."

The first mate stopped and turned to John. "This is the last slaving trip I'm making," he said quietly. "It's evil we're doing here, even if it's legal. I pray that God will forgive me." Then he walked out, leaving John speechless for once.

The wind was growing in strength when John came on night watch. A few stars flickered in a patch of southern sky, but to the north bolts of lightning flashed from dark heavens. Making the rounds of the top deck, his steps faltered at the ship's increased pitching and rolling.

"Lower the mainsail, mates!" the captain bellowed over the howling wind. "You, there, sailor: help them out," he added, pointing to John.

John struggled with the lines of the huge mainsail. The ship's pitching and rocking grew worse. Waves swept onto the deck. John staggered, then slipped and fell, careening against the rail. Other sailors slid and sprawled around him.

Out of the darkness a mountain of water slammed into John, choking and gagging him and nearly hurling him overboard. A bolt of fear shot through him.

"Tie yourselves down with ropes!" yelled the captain from the bridge.

John lashed himself to a wooden mast, his legs trembling. He'd never seen a storm like this. *We're going to sink*, he thought in a panic. *We'll all drown.* The ship lurched and pitched wildly as the waves slammed into it. The wind shrieked and tore at John. Jagged streaks of lightning shot through the sky, follow by deafening cracks of thunder. Another wall of water poured over the deck. Gasping for breath, he cried out, "Oh, God, help me!"

As he clung to the mast, a sudden memory came to him: John was six years old, and his mother was standing near his bed. It was the very year she had died. He saw her face bending over him, heard her voice saying, "Johnny, my boy, God loves you so much that he sent his son Jesus to die for your sins."

How can God love me? John thought, pushing away the memory.

The side of the ship plunged deep beneath the waves. This time it stayed half-submerged for what seemed an eternity. Water swamped the deck, nearly drowning John, before the ship righted itself.

"We're going to sink! We're going to sink!" John cried out in terror. Suddenly he remembered the slaves in the hold below. *They'll drown, too*, he thought. He felt an impulse to go and help them. "No!" he said aloud. "I'll only drown down there." But the impulse came again.

Grudgingly, he untied the rope around his waist and freed himself from the mast. Creeping along the deck, dodging waves that continued to pour over the ship, he found the stairs and crawled down. The ship rocked suddenly, and he was thrown off the last step. John went spinning into a wall of the lower deck, cracking his head. At last he reached the hold. Dark water swirled around his feet as he felt for the door. It was unlocked!

He peered inside and saw the first mate with a lantern in his hand. He looked up at John. "Come and help me, man!" he shouted. "They'll drown if we don't get them up on deck!"

John waded through the rising water, unchaining the slaves and pushing them toward the door. A curious calm came over him, even as the water reached his waist. He watched the last slave escape to the upper deck, followed by the first mate and his lantern.

By now the water was chest high. *What's happening to me?* John wondered. *I don't feel afraid. I could drown right here, yet I'm at peace. I'm feeling . . . love.*

Then John made his way to the upper deck, still engulfed by this strange sensation. The ship's pitching and rolling was less severe now. The rain had eased up, and stars were breaking through the clouds. John heard the captain order sailors to bail out water from the hold.

Exhausted, he staggered to the ship's bow and wedged himself between two lifeboats to rest. Again he heard his mother's voice: "John, Jesus loves you."

Tears streamed down his face. "I'm sorry, Jesus," he wept. "I'm sorry for all my sins. For everything. Please forgive me."

At that moment, John heard the crack of a whip. He turned to see a man whipping the slaves as he rounded them up. The man cocked his arm for another strike when John caught him by the wrist.

"Easy now, mate," said John. "No need to treat these people like animals. They're human beings, you know. The same as you and me."

The sailor's jaw dropped, and he lowered the whip. "What's gotten into you, John? You never talked like this before."

John looked up at the starlit sky and smiled. "This storm was a blessing in disguise. It taught me an important lesson. Let me tell you about God's amazing grace . . ."

John and all his shipmates were saved from the terrible storm. In later years, God guided him to become an Anglican minister in a town near London. Influenced by John Wesley, the Rev. Newton was determined not to put on airs as he ministered to others. He wore his old seaman's jacket when he made frequent house calls, often singing hymns with the families he visited.

Sometime in the 1760s, he wrote the words to one of the most beloved hymns of all time, "Amazing Grace," which describe the great truth he discovered during that storm at sea. Putting his new understanding of God's love and grace into action, John worked with the anti-slavery leader William Wilberforce to eventually make slavery illegal in England.

Talk about It

- How did the storm change John Newton into a different person? Why do you think it took a storm to "open John's eyes" to God's grace? Can you think of any "storms" that have helped draw you closer to God?

- Read, listen to, or (better) sing together John Newton's famous hymn "Amazing Grace." Talk about the words and how they make you feel. Why do you think this hymn is so very popular with so many people?

Amazing Grace

Amazing grace, how sweet the sound,
That saved a wretch like me!
I once was lost, but now am found,
Was blind, but now I see!

'Twas grace that taught my heart to fear,
And grace my fears relieved.
How precious did that grace appear,
The hour I first believed!

To Fight for the Lord

PETER CARTWRIGHT
1785–1872

As a teenager in the frontier backwoods of America, Peter Cartwright led a pretty wild life—racing horses, carrying six-shooters, and drinking hard. But when Cartwright was sixteen, God gave him a new start. Attending a church service with his mother, Peter heard about the peace and love that Jesus Christ can bring. He confessed his sins in an old-fashioned altar call and accepted Jesus as his Savior.

A Methodist preacher saw the potential in this rough and ready young man and suggested that he study for the ministry. Instead of going to school, Peter took courses by mail, and he got practical experience by assisting circuit-riding Methodist ministers. Each minister had his own circuit, or route, to cover on horseback. Peter rode along, visiting families in frontier territories of Kentucky, Tennessee, Maryland, and Illinois, where no churches were yet built.

Once Peter became a preacher, he did his circuit riding alone, spending many lonely nights on a bedroll under the stars, with mosquitoes and bad weather for company.

PETER ANGLED HIS BLACK AND WHITE SPOTTED APPALOOSA down a turn in the trail. The next settlement lay some miles ahead through the thick pine forests. Peter's mount was exhausted from the long journey. The horse wasn't the only one who was tired. Peter nodded in the saddle, and his stomach growled with hunger.

He was making his rounds as preacher for a sizable circuit covering much of Kentucky. Today he aimed to reach the Crockett homestead where he'd lead an evening worship service. He looked forward to visiting a dozen families he hadn't seen for two months.

Peter smiled as he recalled the strange turn life had taken since his rowdy teenage years. *God must surely love sinners if he can call someone like me to preach*, he thought. Now in his early twenties, he was a full-fledged circuit rider and preacher.

Suddenly the timber trail opened onto a lush meadow. He recognized a cluster of log cabins scattered around the edges of cleared land. The Crockett clan and their neighbors had banded together to stake out this piece of wilderness.

Smoke drifted lazily out of chimneys and the smell of meat roasting on cooking fires filled the air. Peter yelled a greeting as he hitched his Appaloosa to a tree, then he grinned as Crockett children poured out of their house to swarm around him.

"It's the preachy man!" shouted Sammy, Ben Crockett's youngest son.

"Hey, Sammy. Howdy there, Shawna. Jeremy, you get bigger by the month!" Peter greeted the children. They laughed with glee and followed him to the door of their father's cabin.

Bending his head to avoid hitting the low doorway, Peter entered the log cabin. The aroma of baked beans and pork greeted him, making his mouth water.

"Brother Peter, welcome!" called Ben, jumping up from a rocking chair. "You're just in time for some pork n' beans."

"Hello, Brother Peter," sang out Martha Crockett from the stove. "Pull up a chair. You children go wash up."

The children scurried off as Peter and Ben pulled up chairs to the table.

When the children returned, Peter gave thanks to God for the food Martha had laid out before them. Then all talk stopped while everyone filled their plates and stomachs. The children giggled as they watched Peter put down huge portions of everything in sight.

At last he sat back in his chair and sighed with contentment. "Forgive me for not talking much. Nobody lays on a spread like Martha. Now I guess I'm ready for anything!"

"You may have to be," said Ben grimly. "There's a bunch of good-for-nothin' varmints that rode in yesterday and camped over in the woods. Last night they whooped and hollered and drank 'til dawn. I went over and asked them to calm down, but they just cursed me. I think they aim to make trouble at the service tonight. Some of the families here are wondering if we shouldn't just call off the service."

"What?" Peter cried. "We can't let a bunch of drunks keep us from worshiping the Lord!"

Ben smiled. "Hear that, Martha? Nothing's gonna stop young Peter here from telling folks about Jesus."

"Praise the Lord!" exclaimed Martha. "But what are we going to do if those men make trouble?"

"Well, let's ask the Lord to help us think ahead a little," said Peter. "And maybe they won't bother us at all."

After dinner Peter and Ben set up wooden benches near the largest cabin. In front of the benches they placed a rough plank across two sawhorses and covered it with a white cloth. This would serve as the altar. After lighting torches on several posts, Ben clanged an old bell to sound assembly for worship.

Men, women, and children—about fifty of them—began filling the wooden benches. Martha had already started playing a lively hymn on her accordion. People joined in singing, some clapping their hands.

When the people were seated, Peter stood before the altar and began a prayer. But before he could finish, a tall, bearded man came swaggering up the aisle between the benches. Catcalling and whistling, he held a jug of whiskey in one hand and a tightly coiled bullwhip in the other. His friends moved up behind the group, grinning as they watched.

Peter's prayer trailed off, and his eyes widened as the man neared the altar. He put his Bible down, grabbed the man by the shoulder, and spun him around. "Sir, you are in the Lord's house," he said. "You will show some respect."

"Oh, yeah?" sneered the man. His breath reeked of whiskey. "I don't see no Lord. And I don't see no church."

The man's friends snickered. Several started moving up the aisle as well. "That's tellin' 'em, Lukas!" shouted one of them.

Peter had a firm grip on the man's shoulder, when suddenly the bearded man spun around and struck Peter with his whip.

Peter reached for Lukas's whip, but Lukas was too quick. He stepped back and hit Peter in the stomach, this time with a fist.

Peter lurched back, stunned for several seconds. Then his face grew red with fury. "Lord," he said, "forgive me for what I am about to do." He cocked his long arm and snapped it forward, catching Lukas square on the chin with a mighty blow.

"Hooray for the preachy man!" yelled little Sammy before his mother could shush him.

Lukas reeled from the blow. Dropping his whip and bottle, he fell flat on his face.

Peter snatched the whip from the ground and used it to tie Lukas's hands. Just as three of Lukas's friends started to rush Peter, the men of the Crockett camp moved in. Faced with superior numbers, they disappeared back into the forest, leaving their friend to fend for himself.

Peter asked Ben and the others to prop up Lukas on a bench in the front row. When he came to and saw that his friends had deserted him, Lukas cursed under his breath but offered no struggle.

Peter picked up his Bible from the ground, dusted it off, and resumed his position in front of the altar.

"Sorry, folks," he said. "Seems like every now and then the devil wants to get his two cents worth in at these meetings. But we're just not buying it."

One of the women piped up, "But Brother Peter, didn't Jesus tell us to turn the other cheek? Didn't he say that those who live by the sword die by the sword?"

Peter stopped in his tracks. *Those are good questions*, he thought. *Maybe I shouldn't have hit the man.*

He gave Lukas a studied look. Then he walked over and knelt down to untie the man's hands. "Lukas," he said, "I came here to tell people about the love of God and ended up fighting. I reckon that's how I used to handle things, but I don't want to go back to those ways."

Lukas stared at Peter distrustfully, but he stayed in his seat and kept listening to the preacher's words.

Then Peter stood up and turned to the silent congregation. "I want to tell everybody here that even though I'm a preacher of the gospel, I'm still a sinner saved by grace. I drank and fought and cussed a good bit in my younger years, before the Lord got me by the collar and filled me with his love. And I thought I'd changed." He turned to Lukas. "I want to apologize for whacking you upside the head, Lukas."

Lukas stood up, his head lowered and his feet shuffling. "Now that I'm sobered up some," he admitted, "I reckon I'll say I'm sorry for wrecking your service. I ain't never been to church. I think I'll stay awhile, if you don't mind." He sat down and took off his hat.

Peter nodded and smiled. "The Bible says we've all sinned and fallen short of God's perfection. We're all bad in our own way. God sent Jesus to die on the cross for our sins. Now we can be friends of God and stop hurting each other. That's what I came to say tonight. And I guess God gave us the best sermon illustration I ever did see."

Peter turned around and faced the makeshift altar. "Anyone who wants to," he invited, "come on up here and kneel with me." Peter knelt down and folded his hands in prayer. Quiet footsteps brought fifteen people to their knees by Peter's side.

And one of them was Lukas.

*P*eter Cartwright was one of the foremost churchmen of the new American West. His straightforward honesty and strength of purpose helped him lead many people to the Lord. He was a presiding elder of the Methodist church for over fifty years. In his later years, Peter also served in the Illinois legislature and even ran against Abraham Lincoln for Congress.

Talk about It

- When Peter Cartwright became a Christian, he got to wipe the slate clean and begin a new life, using his energy to do God's will. But being a Christian doesn't make us perfect. What do you think about the way Peter handled the rowdy men? How else could they have been handled? Is it ever right to show your anger? Is it ever right to use physical force against someone?

- Can you think about times you've lost your temper with friends or a family member? How did those times turn out for you and for the person with whom you got angry? What is the best way to apologize when you have lost your temper?

Prayer

Dear Lord, our family needs your wisdom in everything we do. We know we are humans who are also sinners, but you love us anyway. When we make mistakes, help us admit them quickly and learn to make amends. Help us to be as forgiving of others as you are forgiving of us. Amen.

Standing up for Truth

SOJOURNER TRUTH
1797–1883

Sojourner Truth was an African-American woman who stood up for truth. She refused to let the fact that she was born a slave keep her down. Once she gained her freedom, Sojourner became a tireless speaker for the abolition of slavery and for women's rights. In 1851 she gave one of her most famous speeches at a women's rights meeting.

Sojourner Truth was born with the slave name Isabella in the state of New York. After coming to know God and finding freedom, she adopted the name Sojourner Truth.

As a slave, Isabella—or "Bell," as she was known—worked for a cruel man named Dumont. She had five children, whom Dumont sold to other slave owners. Finally, Bell got up courage to run away. She sought refuge in the home of a Quaker family, the Van Wageners. They purchased Bell from Dumont and then freed her. Bell chose to take their name—Van Wagener—as her own, and to work for them as a housekeeper. But her heart was troubled about her children, especially her six-year-old son, Peter.

"Dumont sold Little Peter?!" Bell exclaimed, fury and despair rising within her.

"Yes, Bell. We heard today. Your old master sold Peter to an owner from Alabama," said Mrs. Van Wagener quietly, placing her hand on Bell's broad shoulder.

"But he can't! I mean, he can't do that, can he?" Bell protested, tears flooding her eyes. "Isn't it against the law to sell a slave out of New York State?"

The gentle Quaker woman nodded. "Yes, it is against the law, Bell. But you'd have to file a lawsuit against Dumont and the Alabama owner. It's unheard of for a Negro to do that."

Bell set her jaw. She stood up to her full six feet and raised her eyes toward heaven. "Jesus," she prayed, "you are my Master now, my Good Master. Help me get my boy Peter back from Alabama."

"Amen," Mrs. Van Wagener agreed quietly. "It seems impossible, but may God guide your steps, Bell."

At bedtime, Bell went up to her room and knelt by her cot. "Father in heaven," she prayed, "I want to try to walk in your truth. I'm a free woman now, but my son Peter is a slave. Give me courage to get him back home with me so he can know freedom, too."

The next day, Bell arose early and put on a white bonnet and a long black dress. Wrapping a shawl around her shoulders, she set out on the dusty road to the town of Kingston. On the edge of the Hudson River, she found the courthouse that Mr. Van Wagener had described to her. The clerk she spoke with was astonished at Bell's bold request, but he completed the paperwork for filing a lawsuit.

"In two days, you will have to appear before a grand jury," the clerk told her, setting a time for the appearance.

Bell found a nearby rooming house where she waited for her day in court. Two days later, she marched up the steps of the courthouse, ready to talk to somebody called a grand jury.

I have to find a grand person and tell him my story, she said to herself as she looked around. She noticed a well-dressed man walking through the hall. *How grand he looks. That must be the person!* she thought, hurrying up to him.

"Sir," she said politely, "I need to tell about my boy Peter and how he was sold against the law to a master in Alabama . . ."

"Who are you supposed to tell?" asked the man.

"Why, a grand jury, sir. Aren't you a grand person?"

The man smiled kindly. "No," he said, "you need to go to the grand jury courtroom. It's the first room down the hall."

"I thank you, sir," said Bell. She hurried down the hallway, filled with certainty that she would get Peter back.

In the courtroom, the judge glanced over the papers of her lawsuit and then called her to the stand. The grand jury, made up of a dozen somber men, sat in two rows facing Bell.

"Isabella Van Wagener," said the judge, "please tell me and the grand jury why you filed this lawsuit."

Bell faced the jury. In a deep, powerful voice, she addressed the twelve men: "My little boy, Peter—he's just six years old—was sold by my old master here in New York to a master in Alabama. Now that is against the law, and it's wrong," she declared. "And by God's grace, I want him brought back here to New York right away."

The judge asked more questions as he flipped through the papers. Finally, he looked up at Bell and sighed. "I am sorry, Miss Van Wagener," he said, "but the laws of two states are at issue here. You are going to need a good lawyer. Without a good lawyer, I'm afraid you won't get your son back."

Bell trudged back along the street to the rooming house, her heart heavy, her head bowed. "Why didn't you help me, Lord?" she asked. "I felt so sure you were with me."

She looked up to see a man walking toward her. A small voice spoke within her: "Don't give up. Ask this man for help."

Bell stopped the man and urgently told him her problem.

He rubbed his chin thoughtfully. "I know of a good lawyer. His name is Herman Romeyn," he said. "Maybe he can help."

Bell rushed back into town to the lawyer's office.

"All right, Isabella Van Wagener," said Romeyn, after she told him her story. "I'll do my best to get your boy back quickly. But my fee is five dollars."

"I don't have any money, Mr. Romeyn," she exclaimed. Then she thought for a moment and added, "But I'll raise the five dollars and bring it tomorrow."

"I know you are leading the way, Lord," Bell exulted on her way to the rooming house. "But how in the world can I come up with five dollars?"

As she walked up the rooming house steps, that small voice spoke up again: "Ask for help from people in this house."

Bell scurried from room to room, explaining to each person that she needed five dollars to get her boy back. By the end of the night, she had much more than five dollars.

The next morning, Bell returned to the lawyer's office. "Here is your money, Mr. Romeyn," she said eagerly, handing him a fistful of bills.

"But this is much more than five dollars," he protested.

"I aim to give you all I collected so you'll work with all your might to get my son back," she explained. She paused, then she asked, "Can I come and pick up Peter tomorrow evening?"

Romeyn smiled. "I'm afraid it will take a little longer than that, Isabella," he said.

Finally, the lawyer had good news. "Tomorrow morning, your son Peter will be in court, along with the Alabama slave owner and his lawyer," he informed her. "I will do my best to return him to you."

The next morning, Bell paced back and forth in the back of the courtroom as the judge heard the two lawyers present their arguments. Her son sat huddled in a chair next to the Alabama slave owner. He wouldn't look at her. He stared down at the floor, not moving a muscle.

The judge noticed the boy's fearful behavior and said, "Peter, you may go sit with your mother if you wish."

To everyone's surprise, Peter shouted out, "She's not my mother!" He began howling, "I don't want to leave my master. He's good to me."

Bell felt as though a knife had stabbed her heart.

The judge looked skeptically at the slave owner, then he looked at the boy. "Come to me, Peter," he said gently.

Peter dragged his feet as he approached the bench. The judge got down from the platform, knelt in front of the boy, and looked at him carefully. "This boy is trembling with fear," the judge said. "I believe he was threatened by his master."

The judge led Peter back to his chair and returned to the bench, glaring at the slave owner. Gavel in hand, he declared: "I hereby award the boy Peter to his mother, Isabella Van Wagener." He banged the gavel and added, "By the way, Miss Van Wagener, you have made history today. You are one of the first Negroes to have won a court case in these United States."

Bell ran over and swept Peter into her arms. "Oh, Lord, thank you, thank you!" she cried out. "Judge, God bless you. Mr. Romeyn, God bless you!"

Peter hugged his mother and buried his face in her neck.

That night Bell and Peter were welcomed home by the Van Wageners. At bedtime, Bell bathed Peter, moaning when she saw the whip scars that lined his back. She tucked him gently into a second cot the Van Wageners had provided.

"Mama?" Peter asked timidly.

"Yes, my child," replied Bell.

"The slave owner told me he'd beat me somethin' terrible if I didn't say those things," he confessed.

"I know, my son," she said. "But you're safe with me now. You'll never be a slave again. Jesus loves you dearly, and so do I."

*L*ater, Bell left the Van Wageners and went to New York with her two youngest children. Here she supported herself as a housekeeper and began working and preaching in the streets of the city. In 1843, she left New York and took the name Sojourner Truth, which she used from then on. She felt called to become a wandering evangelist—a sojourner who carried the truth about God to everyone she met. She preached and sang about Christian love and tolerance at prayer meetings, churches, and meeting halls throughout the land. Some years later, Sojourner appeared in court one more time. A group of rowdies had dislocated her shoulder by manhandling her for speaking on the abolition of slavery. She sued them and won again!

Sojourner Truth fiercely believed in justice, freedom, and equality under God. Alive with her sense of God's love, she spoke God's truth freely, whether to the poor and needy or to President Lincoln himself.

Talk about It

- A sojourner is someone who stops or stays in a place for only a short time and then moves on. And truth—God's truth that everybody is equal and loved—was something Bell strongly believed in and practiced. So her new name, Sojourner Truth, fit her well. What qualities are most important to you in your life? If you were to choose a name that showed what you believe in and who you are, what would it be?

- What was there about Sojourner Truth that made her successful in acting and speaking out against prejudice and injustice? Do you think those qualities are as effective in battling prejudice today?

Prayer

Dear Jesus, give us courage to show and teach love and justice to one another. Help us speak up for truth today—and help us speak the truth to those who need to hear it. Teach us your way, Lord, that we may walk in your truth.

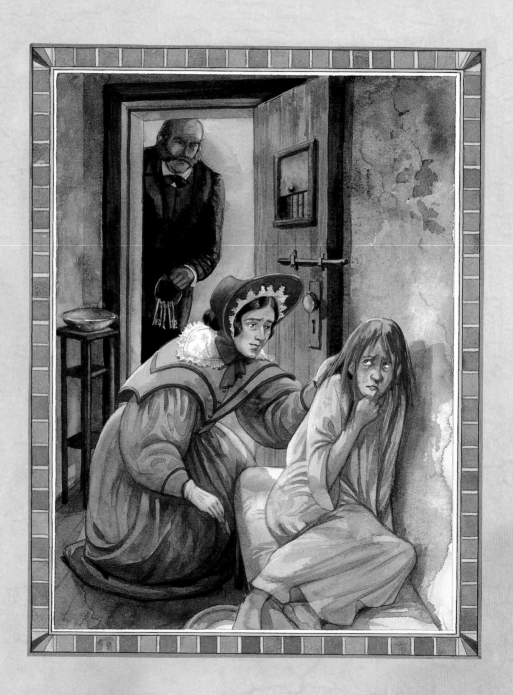

A Lady of Courage and Kindness

DOROTHEA LYNDE DIX
1802–1887

*A*t a time when it was considered improper for "ladies" to be involved in such things, Dorothea Dix almost single-handedly brought reform to the treatment of mentally ill people in the United States.

Dorothea was born into poverty in backwoods New England. Her parents believed children needed punishment in order to grow up as good Christians, and they practiced that belief with their own children.

In her teens, Dorothea left home to live with her wealthy grandmother in Boston. Relieved of her own poverty, she embarked on a life of service to the poor and oppressed. In Boston, she started a private school and spent all her free time tutoring poor children.

Eventually, too much work brought on illness and severe depression, and Dorothea was forced to rest. Friends invited her to spend time in England, where she slowly recovered. During her stay, she was taken to visit a new hospital for mentally ill people. Dorothea was impressed by the quality of care offered at the hospital, and she remembered that visit many years later, after she returned to America.

DOROTHEA DIX MARCHED DOWN THE HALL-
WAY of the Massachusetts State Assembly
House. Portraits of male legislators hanging on
the walls seemed to scowl down upon her, a
lone woman in these halls of men.

Tucking a strand of hair back into her bonnet and straightening her long gray dress, she
knocked firmly on Assemblyman Harris's office door.

"Come in," commanded a gruff voice.

Dorothea entered the dark, paneled office. Mr. Harris stood up
behind his desk and nodded abruptly to her.

"You are prompt, Miss Dix; I'll give you that. Come with me."
He guided her down a long hallway to an antechamber of the
assembly hall. "The legislators are busy men, Miss Dix. I have
promised them your report will be brief."

"I shall speak to the point, Mr. Harris," Dorothea assured him.
"I appreciate the assembly's willingness to hear about the conditions of the mentally ill in Massachusetts."

Harris opened the door of the assembly room and turned to
her. "Wait here for a few moments," he instructed. "I will return
for you when they are ready."

Dorothea paced back and forth. "Dear God," she whispered,
"please guide my words to these legislators. Open their hearts to
my message. Something must be done to help those poor, unfor-
tunate people in prisons and hospitals."

Dorothea knew it was highly unusual for a woman to be
involved in state affairs. Yet her persistence and her prayers had
finally resulted in a hearing with the all-male assembly.

The door to the meeting room opened again. Harris ushered
Dorothea into the assembly chambers. The men grew silent as they
stared at this bold woman.

Dorothea pulled her report from the folder and placed it on the
speaker's podium. Then she looked out at the assembly.

"Gentlemen, I thank you for your time today. Over the past months, I have visited every prison and house for the poor in Massachusetts. And let me say that I have discovered inhumane conditions—shocking conditions—intolerable to me as a Christian woman and a resident of the state of Massachusetts.

"Mentally ill men and women are jailed with criminals. No distinction is made between those who have committed violent crimes and those who suffer from mental illness.

"Mentally disturbed men and women are forced to live like animals in terrible conditions. They are kept in bare, unheated cells in the freezing cold of winter. When I questioned a jailer about this practice, he told me: 'Lunatics do not feel the cold.'"

Whispers and murmurs rippled through the room.

Dorothea waited for silence, then continued: "These inmates are often bound with chains and ropes. They are fed poorly, often left unclothed, and kept in the dark for long periods of time. The men and women are forced to live in horrible filth."

A steady stream of gasps and exclamations punctuated Dorothea's description of what her visits had uncovered.

Assemblyman Harris thanked Dorothea. "What you tell us has indeed shocked us, as you can see," he concluded. We will certainly talk about this horrible situation." Then he asked, "Do you have any recommendations, Miss Dix?"

Dorothea stood straight and tall. "I recommend that the state of Massachusetts establish separate institutions for persons who are mentally ill," she said. "In these asylums, people can be treated as patients—not criminals—and be cared for with respect for their humanity."

Dorothea walked out onto the Boston street exhausted yet elated at the legislators' interest in her report. She had worked night and day for many months, visiting institutions in every part of Massachusetts, asking questions, making notes, and writing up her findings for this report. In the words of the Bible, she was determined to "bring good news to the poor . . . proclaim release to the captives . . . let the oppressed go free."

Now it was time for a little extravagance, she decided. Hailing a horse-drawn cab for her journey home, Dorothea collapsed against the soft leather cushions and closed her eyes. "Thank you, God," she prayed, "for being in the assembly today. I know that you care about the mentally ill. Please inspire the legislators to follow my recommendations."

The horse trotted through the streets to her grandmother's large home. For the first time in weeks Dorothea relaxed. Suddenly she noticed that trees were budding, daffodils were blooming. "Why, I almost missed spring!" she said aloud.

When she entered her grandmother's house, a maid told her that a visitor was waiting in the library. Hurrying in, she saw her best friend, Henrietta, standing by the window.

"Dorothea!" cried Henrietta, running to embrace her. "I couldn't wait to find out how the legislators responded."

"They were properly shocked," declared Dorothea. "They listened and then asked for my recommendations."

"Wonderful. Wonderful. You have done a splendid thing." Then Henrietta stepped back and looked carefully at Dorothea. "You are looking quite pale, my dear," she said. "Now that this burden is off your shoulders, I hope you will take time to rest, to regain your strength."

Dorothea sighed and smiled at her friend. "This is only the start of it, Henrietta," she said. "From what I am discovering about legislators, worthy causes can get lost in politics."

The next evening, Dorothea attended a dinner party at a church member's home. At the table, she sat next to one of the church deacons who had helped arrange for her speech to the legislators. She nodded to Assemblyman Harris, who was seated farther down the long table.

"I hear your speech yesterday caused quite an uproar in the legislature, Miss Dix," said the deacon, his eyes twinkling.

"I want to thank you for helping make it possible," Dorothea replied. "I just hope and pray that action will be taken."

After dinner, Assemblyman Harris approached Dorothea over coffee in the parlor. "Miss Dix," he said, "I must tell you there is discussion about whether the conditions you described are entirely accurate."

Dorothea felt her temper rising. "Why is that so, may I ask?"

"It seems that Mr. Curtis, one of our new assemblymen, shares your interest in prison conditions. But in his own research, he did not find the problems you described."

"Indeed?" snapped Dorothea. "Perhaps Mr. Curtis would like to join me on a tour of every jail I visited. How did he conduct his own research?"

"Why don't you ask him right now?" suggested Harris. "Mr. Curtis is here this evening." He beckoned for a dark-haired young man to join them. "Miss Dix, meet Mr. Curtis."

"How do you do, Mr. Curtis," Dorothea said icily.

"Miss Dix asked me how you conducted your research, Mr. Curtis," said Harris. "Perhaps you would tell us both."

"Certainly," Curtis replied. "My assistants and I interviewed men in charge of jails. They indicated that some improvements were needed but nothing on the scale suggested by Miss Dix."

"Did you yourself examine the areas where prisoners were kept?" Dorothea asked sharply.

Curtis looked annoyed. He shook his head. "Actually, no. I saw no need to distrust the jail officials."

"I had to fight with those officials at every jail I visited so I could see how the prisoners lived!" Dorothea exclaimed. "In some cases, I ignored their protests and walked past the men."

Curtis's face reddened. He said nothing.

Mr. Harris smiled. "Miss Dix, I commend your boldness. Your actual observations speak for themselves. I will recommend that the legislature fund your proposals for building asylums for the mentally ill."

Several weeks later, Harris invited Dorothea back to his office. As she entered, he stood up and took her hand. "I'm delighted to tell you that the legislature has passed the proposals you recommended. We have authorized funds to start construction of the first asylum. And the assembly has asked that you act as advisor for the project."

That night as she knelt by her bed, Dorothea prayed: "Thank you, God. Now the real work begins."

*D*orothea Dix repeated in other states the approach she had used successfully in Massachusetts. In 1841, when she began her work, there were thirteen mental asylums in the United States. In 1880, after her efforts of lobbying state and federal politicians, as well as advising on the building and operation of many facilities, there were 123 asylums—twenty-three of which she helped to operate or acted as an advisor for.

In addition to her compassionate ministry to mentally ill people, Dorothea Dix served as a superintendent of nurses during the Civil War, helping to oversee care of the wounded and dying. She died in 1887.

Talk about It

- Dorothea Dix must have had a hard childhood filled with poverty and ruled by parents who practiced punishing discipline. One might expect that when she moved to the comfort and wealth of her grandmother's home, she would turn her back on poverty. Instead, she spent her life helping poor and oppressed people. Do you know people like Dorothea Dix—people whose bad experiences have made them kind and caring? Do you know others whose hard lives have made them angry and resentful? What do you think accounts for such a difference?

- It is one thing to feel empathy for those less fortunate than we. It is another to do something about it. What realistic activities could your family undertake to help less fortunate persons?

Prayer

Dear Father, help our family grow in kindness and compassion to each other and to people who are less fortunate than we. Help us put our love for you into actions for others. Amen.

The Boy Who Read with His Fingertips

LOUIS BRAILLE
1809–1852

Can you imagine opening your eyes and seeing nothing but darkness, even in daylight? Darkness everywhere? All the time?

Born in a small French village outside Paris, Louis (LOO-ee) Braille (BRAYL) went blind at the age of three, accidentally injuring himself while playing with his father's tools. This was a time before seeing-eye dogs or books for the blind. If they were lucky, blind people might learn a trade; more often they were doomed to begging on the streets.

It was unusual for a blind child to attend school. Yet when a kindly priest convinced the local teacher to take Louis as a student, the youngster soon was at the head of his class.

In 1819, Louis went to live and study at the National Institute for the Blind in Paris, where he stayed for the rest of his life.

Louis Braille became a blessing for blind people around the world. With his one invention, Louis improved forever the lives of blind people, and he did so at the tender age of fifteen!

SEVEN-YEAR-OLD LOUIS tapped his wooden cane on the cobblestones as he felt his way up the hilly street. He was on his way to see his friend Father Palluy (pall-WHEE). The priest lived in a house next to the old village church. Using the cane his father had made, Louis felt proud that he was walking by himself.

Louis hated to recall the accident that had blinded him several years earlier. He had been playing with leather scraps on the floor of his father's harness shop. His father had warned him never to touch the sharp tools hanging high above his head.

That day, a customer came in and distracted Louis's father's attention. Louis gazed up at the shiny tools, wondering if he could punch holes into leather the way his father did. The urge grew irresistible. Climbing onto the worktable, he unhooked a tool from the wall. Suddenly he missed his step and, as he fell to the floor, the tool stabbed his eye.

His parents rushed him to a local healer who treated and then bandaged the bloody eye. Unfortunately, both eyes became infected. One morning several days after the accident, Louis awoke to a world of darkness. He had gone completely blind.

Louis could tell he had reached the top of the hill when he felt the street grow level beneath his feet. He walked farther, until sounds made by his tapping cane told him he'd reached the iron gate of Father Palluy's house.

Father Palluy answered his knock on the door. "Welcome, Louis! I've been expecting you."

With his left hand on the priest's arm, Louis accompanied Father Palluy into the carpeted study and sat down beside him.

"I got here all by myself," Louis said proudly. "I looked with my ears and my feet and my cane!"

"You're a brave boy, Louis. And God is with you," replied Father Palluy.

Louis lowered his head. "Yes, Father," he said, "but sometimes I feel very lonely."

"I understand," the priest said. "But you are doing well at school. I hear good reports from your teacher."

"Yes," Louis said. A smile quickly replaced his downcast look. "I like school very much. A kind girl reads me the texts each day. And I listen carefully to what the teacher says."

"You use your memory well, even though you cannot read."

Louis again looked sad for a moment, then asked, "Can you tell me if there are books in this room, Father?"

"Why yes, Louis. There are many books that I've collected from my studies." The priest stood up. "Come. I'll show you." He guided Louis to the large wooden bookcase.

Louis reached out both hands and began touching the books. He caressed the spines and the soft covers. He pulled books close to his nose and sniffed the leather covers and the musty pages. Taking a book off the shelf, he opened it and ran his fingers over a page. Suddenly he spread wide his arms and embraced as many books as he could reach.

"Father, I love books!" he cried. "I want to read them all!"

Father Palluy looked thoughtfully at Louis. "Come, sit and pray with me, my son."

"Lord," said Father Palluy, "you know every hair on Louis's head. You know how brave he is about his blindness and about the bullies who tease him. Bless him for his courage. Continue to bless his studies in school. And I pray that one day you will show him a way to read the books he loves so dearly."

Louis's sightless eyes filled with tears. "Oh, yes, Lord God, that is my desire," he whispered.

After a short while the priest's face lit up and he gently touched Louis's arm. "Louis, I believe God will use your blindness for his glory and the good of mankind."

That evening before dinner, Louis sat by the fireplace singing a song he had learned at school. A delicious aroma began to fill the house. He grinned as he recognized the smell. "Chicken stew, Mama! My favorite!"

Even though it was past working hours, Louis could hear his father hammering in the workshop. He walked to the door and called out: "What are you doing, Papa?"

His father continued hammering for a few moments before answering. "I've made something for you, Louis," he replied, walking over and handing his son a square piece of wood.

Louis ran his fingers over the board. "There are nails all over it, Papa!" Louis said. "I count sixteen. What are they for?"

His father smiled and ruffled Louis's curly hair. "I just thought the nails would be fun for you. Maybe you can make up a new game."

The family said grace at the dinner table and dug into the chicken stew. Louis's older brother Henri (ahn-REE) sat opposite him. "What Bible story do you want me to read you tonight, Louis?" he asked.

Louis thought for a moment. "I'd like the story about Joseph and his coat of many colors!" he exclaimed. "I get to imagine what all the colors look like."

"It's one of my favorite stories, too," said his mother. "What else do you like about it?"

"That Joseph was the littlest one of all, but he ended up helping everybody."

At the age of ten, Louis went to live and attend classes at the National Institute for the Blind in Paris. One day, after he'd been at the Institute for five years, Louis was daydreaming during history class.

"Louis," exclaimed the teacher, "Why are you not answering my question? What are you thinking about this time?"

Aroused from his daydream, Louis said. "I'm sorry, Monsieur (muhs-YUR) Gillette (zhee-LET). What did you ask?"

"Please stay after class, Louis," sighed Monsieur Gillette. "I want to speak to you."

After the rest of the students had left the classroom, Louis stood by the teacher's desk.

"Louis, this is not like you, this daydreaming you have been doing lately," said Monsieur Gillette. "You are fifteen—too old for daydreaming." He peered more closely at Louis's tired face. "What are you doing that leaves you so exhausted?"

Louis's head drooped sadly. "I've been trying to figure out how we blind people might be able to read," he said. "Night after night I experiment with different touch patterns for the alphabet. But nothing works. The patterns are too complicated for my fingers to remember."

Monsieur Gillette frowned. "Louis, you should concentrate on what blind people are capable of doing. Reading is not important for the blind. Learning a trade that allows you to support yourself with your blindness—that's what's important."

Louis shuffled back to his dormitory room half-heartedly tapping his cane in front of him. *Maybe Monsieur Gillette is right*, he thought. *Maybe it's a waste of time.*

Later that night Louis sat at his desk, overwhelmed by feelings of discouragement. *I've been working on this problem for over a year*, he thought. *How can I simplify the code?*

Into his despair crept a memory of what Father Palluy had told him years ago: "I believe God will use your blindness for his glory and the good of mankind."

Louis got down on his knees by his bed. "Please help me, God," he prayed. "Show me how blind people can read."

Then, as he lay in bed trying to fall asleep, a new idea sparked fire in his mind. He jumped out of bed and grabbed the wooden board and pointed metal stick with which he'd been working.

Quickly he spread a fresh sheet of paper over the board. *What if I make two rows of three dots each?* he thought.

Louis rapidly punched holes in the paper with the stylus, creating several tiny patterns. Then he turned the paper over and ran his fingertips across the raised bumps.

"Yes!" he whispered. "These patterns are small enough for my fingertips to read quickly."

Experimenting some more, he gave a different six-dot code to each letter of the alphabet. He worked feverishly until he had captured the entire alphabet.

"Now," he said aloud, "let me try writing my name." Louis punched in the code for his name and hurriedly ran his fingers over the bumps.

"'LOUIS BRAILLE'!" he shouted. "I've done it! I can read with my fingers. Oh, thank you, God, for answering my prayers. Now many fingers will see! Now light will fill the darkness!"

*I*n the summer of 1824, when he was fifteen, Louis invented what became known as the Braille system—an alphabet that could speak to the blind. Worldwide libraries for the blind now use his universal language of raised dots on paper. The ability to read and write opened doors for blind persons to share in the written wealth of human learning.

Talk about It

- The writer of the New Testament book of Hebrews (11:34) tells about great biblical heroes who "won strength out of weakness." How was Louis Braille like those biblical heroes? What was there about Louis that helped him turn his blindness into a blessing? How did Louis's family help him cope with his difficulties?

- Take a few moments to think about the "weaknesses" or difficulties in your own lives. Share these with one another. Then talk together about how God—and your family members—might help each of you turn the weakness into a blessing.

Prayer

Dear Lord, we offer you our weaknesses and failures and disappointments. Help us look at each of these in a new way—as an opportunity to turn for help to you and to one another, as a chance to discover new things about you and our family and ourselves. And remind us that you love us always, whether we succeed or whether we fail. Amen.

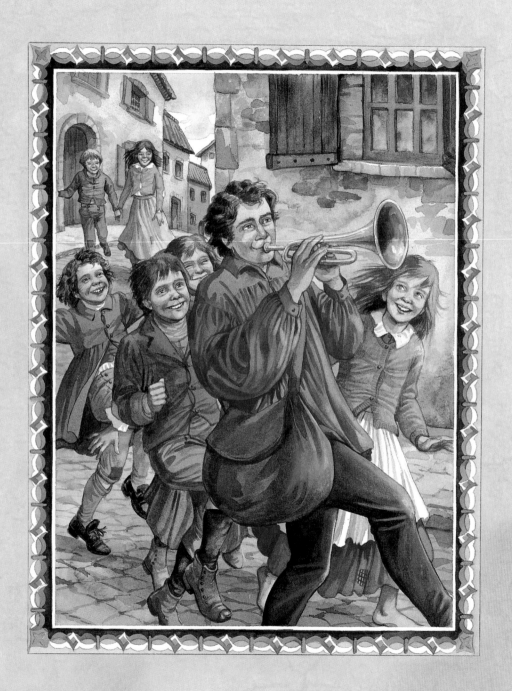

Getting Playful for God

♛

JOHN BOSCO
1815–1888

*I*n the 1800s, the Industrial Revolution changed Europe forever. Many people who had worked on farms moved to towns
and cities. They worked in factories for long hours and little
pay. Often, children got lost in the shuffle. In the Italian town
of Turin, many poor children were abandoned in the streets.

Young John Bosco and his mother moved to Turin from a farm after
John's father died. Mrs. Bosco was hard-working, but she could barely provide for them both. To distract himself from their poverty, John learned gymnastics and theatrical tricks to amuse his friends.

At the age of nine, John had a dream. He was surrounded by children
who were fighting and swearing. Suddenly a beautiful lady appeared and said,
"Softly, softly . . . if you wish to win them! Take your shepherd's staff and
lead them to pasture." As she spoke, the children changed into quiet lambs.

From then on, John knew his calling was to help poor boys and girls. At
sixteen, he decided to become a priest. But how could he reach poor children
and bring them closer to God? Could John's skill in gymnastics and tricks
provide a key?

JOHN BOSCO TRUDGED BACK from the town square to his small room near the church. *Nothing I do with the street children works,* he thought miserably. *When I try to tell them about Jesus, they just scoff and run away.* Flopping down on his cot, he stared up at the ceiling. *Is there another way?* he wondered.

As a child, John had amused friends by turning cartwheels in the street or making pebbles disappear from his hands. He also used such tricks to distract himself from his own hunger. An added benefit was that passersby would often throw coins into his hat.

A young priest had stopped to watch him one day, and the priest talked with John about how the Lord Jesus loved little children. Attracted by this man's kindness, John started slipping into mass at the church. He loved the rainbow colors of the stained glass when the sun shone through them. He didn't understand many of the priests' words, but he felt strangely secure in church, especially when the organ played or when the bread and wine were blessed and served.

The priest who had befriended John noticed that he was a bright child. He selected John and a few other boys to start a small school. John learned to read the Bible and began assisting the priest with mass. He loved reading about how Jesus cared for the poor and how he held young children on his knee.

When he was not helping the priest or attending school, John still liked to play outside, practicing back flips and delighting his friends with tricks of magic.

Now that John was completing seminary training, he felt a burning desire to share Jesus with the street children. And he wanted to find a way to draw them to the church for protection and education. But every time he approached them, the children either yawned or ran away.

John's thoughts were interrupted by the bell for prayer. He jumped up from the cot and joined his classmates in the chapel. As he knelt in prayer, images of Turin's street children came to his mind. "Dear Jesus," he prayed, "can't you please show me a way to reach these children whom you love so dearly? I've tried everything I can think of, and nothing works."

The next afternoon, when his classes were over, John walked to the town square again. His prayer about reaching the street children seemed unanswered. He was beginning to wonder if God had something else in mind for him. Then, as he turned the corner, John stopped in his tracks. A crowd of children had gathered around a man standing on a wooden box. The man wore a blue cape and white gloves. As he waved a wand, the children watched, spellbound and silent. Pouf! In the blink of an eye, a feather turned into a blooming red flower!

Oh, great! thought John. *Here I've been trying to get their attention for months and they ignore me. Now this total stranger comes along and they flock to him.*

Suddenly John heard an inner voice speak through his feelings of annoyance: "Why don't you learn something from this man? What's the matter with having fun with these little ones?"

John frowned for a moment. Then he laughed out loud. And finally he hurried out of the square deep in thought.

Early the next afternoon, John appeared in the square wearing a bright red shirt and carrying a blue cloth bag. He jumped up on the stone fountain and flipped into a headstand. Then he walked around the fountain's edge on his hands. Children laughed as they gathered to watch him.

John turned a series of cartwheels around the fountain, starting off slowly, then flipping faster and faster.

"OOOH!" breathed some of the children. By now, all of them had surrounded John.

Next, John pulled a trumpet from his cloth bag and blew it loudly:Ta-DAH! "The Mighty Bosco will now perform the impossible," he announced. Still on the edge of the fountain, John held out his hands to show that they were empty. Then he leaned over a boy who stood in front. Reaching behind the boy's ear, John pulled out an egg! The astonished children giggled. John balanced the egg carefully on his nose and tiptoed around the fountain's edge.

Suddenly the egg slipped, and the children shrieked in delighted horror. But John's hand swooped down to clasp the egg a mere inch from the cobblestones where it would have splattered. The children applauded uproariously.

John bowed and then motioned for the children to sit. He grew concerned about completing the next part of his plan. "Lord," he whispered, "remember this was your idea—and help me!"

Holding the blue cloth bag up, John asked in a dramatic voice, "What other delights are hidden in the Mighty Bosco's magic bag?" He reached into the bag and began pulling out something golden brown.

"I know!" shouted a little girl. "It's a loaf of bread! May I have some?"

"Me, too!" "I'm hungry, too," chorused other children.

"You'll all get something to eat," John reassured them. "I want anyone ten or older to come up to the front."

A half dozen boys and girls moved forward. John broke the long loaf into six portions and handed a piece to each of the standing children. "Now go back to your seats and share half with a friend."

The children obeyed, but John noticed with alarm that at least a dozen children still had no bread. Desperately, he reached inside the bag and, to his surprise, his fingers felt the crust of a second loaf. His heart skipped a beat as he pulled it out and invited another six children forward to repeat the "bread game."

"This bread is a gift from Jesus," he said, beaming at the children. "God wants us to share it and become his friends."

"Hurrah for Jesus!" called out a little boy, "and hurrah for the Mighty Bosco, too!"

Then John told the story of how Jesus and his disciples fed a huge crowd of people with just a few fish and loaves of bread. The children listened closely. "And do you know that Jesus is here with us today?" John said. "He wants you boys and girls to know how much he loves you."

"Thank you, Jesus," piped up a girl from the back.

"Can you play your trumpet, Mr. Mighty Bosco?" asked a little boy.

"Yes," John said. "I'll be back tomorrow to play my trumpet."

The next afternoon, John returned to the square, his blue bag draped over his shoulder. The moment he arrived, children flocked to him, giggling with glee.

"Good afternoon, my young friends," John sang out. "I invite you to a special event! The Lord Jesus has invited one and all to visit his house." John pulled out his trumpet. After playing a brief fanfare, he shouted, "Follow me!"

Then John marched out of the town square, playing a lively tune. The children rushed after him, forming a long line and imitating John's high-stepping march. The party wound their way down the street toward the church.

At the church doors, John glanced back to see several dozen children. He gathered them into a huddle and said, "Now children, we're going inside to play the quiet game. The quietest one gets to blow my trumpet when we leave." The children grew breathless, each hoping for the chance to blow John's trumpet.

"After we've spent some time with Jesus, we'll go back to the fountain to share more bread. And then I'll teach you how to turn cartwheels!"

The children filed into church, gazing open-mouthed at the stained-glass windows. They filled two pews, fidgeting quietly while they stared at a picture of Jesus, the Good Shepherd.

A smiling priest stepped forward and extended his arms to the group. "Welcome, children," he said kindly. "Welcome to the house of God."

Looking at his little flock of wide-eyed children, John breathed a prayer of gratitude. He smiled as he thought, *The Lord has shown me how to touch their hearts by being playful for God.*

*I*t wasn't long before John had a regular group of children meeting in the church, where they began attending mass. He approached the church and the townspeople for funds to set up schools for boys and girls. He also helped pay for these projects by selling books that he wrote. John was very successful with the children because he used a balance of freedom and discipline—with lots of fun thrown in.

Because John needed dependable assistants to help educate children, he founded a group of priests called the Salesian Order. In 1934, John Bosco was declared a saint by the Roman Catholic Church. "In his life the supernatural almost became the natural and the extraordinary ordinary," said Pope Pius XI of John Bosco.

Talk about It

- Laughing and playing together—enjoying moments of fun with others—is as much God's will as working hard. When does your family feel closest to God: when you are laughing and having fun, or when you are working together? When does your family have the most fun together? How might you expand those times to enjoy each other even more?

- How might you use fun and playfulness to bring a friend or neighbor closer to God?

Prayer

Dear Jesus, we pray for the release of fun and playfulness in our home. Help us relax and enjoy one another as you did when you held the little children on your knee.